Contents

KV-192-278

To my son, David, who is not only an angling pal and willing pupil, but who also did the drawings for this book.

The Book of Angling

Illustrations

AUTHOR'S ACKNOWLEDGEMENT

The author wishes to thank Mr Michael Barrington-Martin
for all the photographs used in the book.

Introduction

I have been angling now, both in freshwater and on the sea, for almost fifty years. To me it seems only yesterday since my first forays after fish: but sadly, I must state that the whole angling scene has changed. And not always for the better. True, we have better tackle and new techniques, but some disturbing elements have crept into the sport.

For example, in this book, which merely sets out to introduce you to the sport, I have made no mention of Record Fishes. Quite recently there was a decision by the British Rod Caught Record Fish Committee to discard certain records – all sorts of rumours grow round this sort of thing – after all, as angling papers report today, it is not unusual for cheating and lying to take place in angling competitions – leads being put into fish, dead fish being netted and put into the weigh-in, even fish caught a day earlier, and then pretended to be caught during the competition. So I am completely disregarding *all* records, but, if you are ever in London, I strongly advise you to see for yourself a truly magnificent carp, *the* record carp, captured by Richard Walker, and alive and well in the London Zoo aquarium. There can be no doubting of that fish, or of the ability of the angler concerned.

I hope in this little book to tell you something about all kinds of fishing so that you can go out and have some real fun. For fishing is fun, there's no doubt about that. It will give you delightful days in summer along lovely streams and rivers, and bring you out in gales along stormswept beaches, and all wild Nature will be there for you to admire. And the fish, too. You will learn their habits, and even sometimes get to know a certain pool or place where one establishes almost a personal relationship with a certain fish!

So if I have helped you in any way, I shall be happy. You

can only take out of sport what you put into it – and you must remember that other people besides anglers have a right to be at the waterside or on it. There are swimmers, and paddlers, and canoeists, and yachtsmen, and water-skiers and skin-divers, too. There is room for all to give and take a little. It is easy to be annoyed if a boat comes in and drags your line off – but there is nothing more hateful than to see grown men, yelling with rage, hurling lead weights and stones at the un-thinking boatman. Don't, I beg of you, follow their example. Angling is known as the contemplative recreation – don't ever let it bring to you envy, malice, or the desire to catch fish merely to win a cup or make money. Let every excursion, however older or experienced you may become, be a happy one.

Hampstead,   Richard Arnold
LONDON.

1 Let's go fishing

'Let's go fishing' is an invitation to one of the finest sports in the world. And particularly if it is the very first invitation one receives to go out and try to catch fish, it might well be the passport to a new world in which fun, good sportsmanship, natural history, and the employment of skills all play their part.

Fishing is fun – there's no doubt about that – and this is well proved by the fact that every weekend in Britain *more* people go fishing than the total number of spectators at professional soccer matches.

What are the attractions of angling?

This is difficult to say because there are so many different things which go to make up an angling day. One of the thrills of angling is that of anticipation. Getting the tackle ready to go out on an angling venture is great fun in itself: selecting the equipment, choosing the bait, checking the reel, and the anticipation of what one is going to catch all build up to a feeling of excitement. Even the journey to the fishing spot, whether a short walk or by train or bus or car, is part of the angling day; the arrival at the waterside is another thrill, followed by setting up the tackle, choosing the place to fish, and finally the fishing itself. It doesn't really matter if one doesn't catch a fish because the whole day is part of angling. Even a most disappointing day can bring fun in discussing with friends what would have happened if one had only changed the bait, or altered the tackle, or moved a hundred yards to another spot, or played the fish more slowly, and so on. 'If' is a great factor in angling. Of course, if one kept going fishing and *never* caught a fish, then the sport would pall and the angler would give up in disgust. Though there could be many reasons for never catching a fish, there are only two main

reasons; either there were no fish in the water, in which case the angler would have been a complete clot to have gone fishing there time after time, or, more likely, he just wasn't using the right tackle, or the right bait, or was fishing at the wrong time: in other words, wasn't fishing properly.

This, then, is a book to try to help you to fish better and to bring to you some of the joys of fishing whether you are going to fish a local pond, or hope to join a club and fish some lake or river, or go down to the coast for sea angling.

Just what is angling? Well, angling is the sport of trying to catch fish using a rod, reel, line, and baited hook. This last item varies, of course, because artificial baits known as 'flies' or 'spoons' or 'spinners' and so on may be used. The principle is the same, though, and the special lure represents something to be eaten.

Fair angling is a term often used and this means that the fish must be properly hooked in the lip or mouth: if the fish should accidentally be hooked in the body, or in a fin, this is termed 'foul-hooking' and fish caught this way cannot be entered into competitions or record lists. Unfortunately, if the fish is terribly greedy, or the angler isn't very skilled, a fish can be allowed to take the baited hook or lure into the throat, or even gorge it. Invariably this means that the fish is badly damaged, cannot fight properly, and if it escapes, or is returned to the water, will probably die. However, though a fish hooked so deeply can be entered for a record list or a competition I feel, and others, too, agree with me that only fish fairly hooked in the mouth or lip should be eligible for competitions, prize lists, or records lists.

There are many different kinds of angling. Straightaway one divides angling into fishing in fresh water and fishing in the sea. But there are other divisions. Freshwater angling is divided into two main groups, coarse fishing and game fishing. This doesn't mean that coarse fish are poor quality fish but it is rather an unfortunate term. The distinction is based on the spawning habits of the fish. So-called coarse fish spawn in the spring months. This is affected by various factors such as temperature and weather conditions and can cover a period from March to the end of May. From 14 March

Plate 1 (*opposite*) Lets go fishing.

13

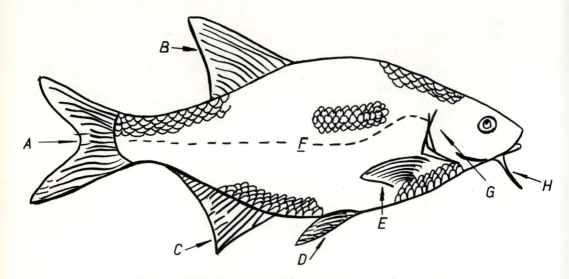

Figure 1 This shows the main physical features of most fishes, though the specimen illustrated does not exist. (A) Caudal fin or tail; (B) Dorsal fin; (C) Anal fin; (D) Pelvic fin; (E) Pectoral fin; (F) Lateral line; (G) Gill cover; (H) Barbule or barbel.

in every year until 16 June the coarse fish enjoy what is termed a 'close' season. During this period one is not allowed to fish for them and the reason behind this is to protect them during their spawning period.

Game fish spawn between October and January, and this can vary according to locality and meteorological conditions.

There are exceptions to both of these rules, however, for the eel, which is regarded as a 'coarse' fish does not spawn during this period, but migrates to the Sargasso Sea for this purpose: and the grayling, which really belongs to the salmon family, and is therefore a 'game fish', spawns at the same time as the 'coarse fish'.

Still dealing with freshwater fishing, perhaps one should consider the two groups I have spoken about. The game fishes comprise members of the salmon family, the migratory trout, trout, char, and the grayling. The coarse fishes are divided into four main groups or families, the perch family, the carp family, the pike family, and the eels. The carp family is a very large family; the carp, barbel, gudgeon, chub, tench, roach, minnow, the bleak, and others are typical members.

Sea fishing is divided into two main groups of fish: big-game fish, such as sharks and tope, and sporting fishes such as the mackerel, the pollack, the cod, and the mullet, to give a few examples. But there is a further distinction in sea fishing according as to whether one fishes from a boat or fishes from the shore.

Though freshwater fishes are protected by fence or close seasons during their breeding periods, there is no such period in sea fishing. The fish spawn at varying times throughout the year and either leave our shores or move elsewhere along the coast.

But whether one fishes in fresh or salt water, seeks game or coarse fish, wishes to battle with a shark, or fish lightly for small harbour smelt, the principles and, in general, the techniques are the same. By learning to use a rod and reel correctly, and to behave properly at the waterside, the angler can go anywhere and catch any fish by varying his skill and techniques according to the circumstances.

In this book, therefore, the techniques and methods common to all forms of angling will be dealt with under a general heading: only when there is a variation to catch a particular species, or accepted method for one branch of angling, will the new approach be dealt with. As for the fishes themselves, let's consider them in the next chapter.

2 Freshwater Fishes

As we saw in Chapter 1 there are two main classes of fish in British waters. The largest group is the coarse fish so we'll deal with that now.

The four main groups I listed were the perch family, the carp family, the pikes, and the eels. Let's deal with them in that order.

The Perch family

These are very handsome fishes and are to be found in all types of fresh water, varying from still waters, such as lakes and ponds, to fast-moving streams and rivers. The perch is a predator, that is, he feeds upon other fishes and insects and small water creatures. Because he is a hunter he is striped like the tiger, with six broad vertical black stripes along his sides. His back, which is humped, is dark olive whilst his sides have a greenish-brown shading of gold, which becomes white underneath. This handsome colour scheme enables him to remain almost invisible against a background of weeds or water plants, like the tiger in the jungle. This has a double purpose as it enables him to hide from foes and at the same time camouflages him when he wants to hunt a victim.

The dorsal fin, the one on his back, has sharp spines so if you catch a perch you have to be very careful how you handle him if you don't want to get gashed. Most lakes hold small perch, and the English Lake District has a wonderful population of perch in Windermere. But where there are too many perch they are invariably very small. A perch of 1 pound in weight is a good catch, but perch over 5 pounds have been caught.

He provides good sport and will take all sorts of bait.

16

Worms, maggots (or gentles), minnows (dead or alive), and artificial lures can all tempt perch on to your hook.

A very much smaller member of the Perch family is the ruffe or pope. In fact he is quite often mistaken for a small perch, but when you think that a large ruffe or pope only weighs about 3 ounces, it is easy to know what you are catching. To identify a pope when you have caught a specimen, look at the dorsal fin. The perch has two separate dorsal fins on his back – the ruffe has his two dorsal fins joined together.

The ruffe is a greedy little fish and can give good sport. But, too, he can be a nuisance if you are fishing seriously for larger perch.

The Carp family

This is a very large and important family of fishes. The ordinary goldfish is a member of the carp family, and although now common in British ornamental ponds and home aquaria, is really a foreigner, coming from China.

The most important member of this family is, of course, the Carp. There are four kinds of carp in British Waters and they range from the *Common Carp,* which grows to an enormous size (the present record fish of 44 pounds, caught by Richard Walker in 1952 is, at the time of writing this book, still alive and on view in the aquarium at the Regent's Park Zoo, in London), the *Mirror Carp,* the *Leather Carp,* and the *Crucian Carp.*

The Common Carp is generally found in lakes, ponds, and gravel pits, but is sometimes to be found in medium and slow-moving rivers. The Common Carp has a short, deep, thick body with a huge mouth. Its colour is generally golden-brown, shading to a yellowish-white underneath. The Mirror Carp is a variation on the Common Carp, but the Leather Carp is easy to identify because to all intents and purposes he has no scales at all. The Common Carp and his near cousins have barbels on the mouth: the Crucian Carp, however, does not have this physical characteristic and it very rarely weighs more than 4 pounds.

The Bream is a member of the Carp family. There are two varieties, the Common (or Bronze) Bream, and the Silver Bream. Their names describe their differences in colour, but the Silver Bream is really more green than silver! Both are hump-backed in appearance because their head is so small in proportion to their bodies. The Silver Bream rarely grows to any size, and is usually caught weighing but ounces. The Bronze Bream, however, grows very much bigger and the best recorded weight of the Bronze is three times heavier than the Silver. They are to be found in still waters and occasionally in rivers. They feed on the bottom and are usually caught on maggots, lobworms, and paste. They are rather poor fighters, however, and they have the disadvantage that when they are caught they give off great quantities of slime. They are very easy to catch when they have been located, and to make a decent bag of them it pays to use a fairly generous ground bait.

Probably the most important member of the carp family is the *Roach*. More roach are caught by freshwater anglers than any other species of fish in Britain though, to be fair, this refers mainly to small roach. Large specimens of roach are sought after, and the fish weighing 2 pounds and more is eagerly angled for.

The Roach is found in ditches, ponds, lakes, and medium and slow-moving waters. He is a graceful fish with a shapely though thick-set body, and a small head. The fins are red, the back is olive or dark green, and the sides are a beautiful silver. The roach is not easy to catch, especially the larger members of the family, because in keenly fished waters he becomes very wary, and suspicious of all but the finest of tackle and properly presented baits.

The most popular bait used for his capture is the maggot, but hemp seed, bread paste, cheese, wasp grubs, and lobworms can be successfully used to bring him into the landing net.

Another very important member of the Carp family is the *Rudd*. This is very similar in looks to the roach and roach and rudd frequently interbreed. You can tell a rudd, however, because it carries golden tints along its back, something which never happens in the roach, and the fins are usually red. The rudd is a shoal fish and is a surface feeder, and in addition to the usual baits which are used for catching roach, the rudd can be fished for by fly fishing.

An active and attractive member of the carp family is the *Dace*. This, too, likes to swim about in shoals but though it is an attractive fish to look at, and very sporting as well, it is by no means a large fish, and gives good sport all through the season.

Earlier I have referred to the Bream. A similar fish in habits, and often found in the same waters, is the *Tench*. It is rather a handsome fish with a deep, short body and it has black fins. It likes still waters, especially lakes and ponds with muddy bottoms and it may be found by the streams of air bubbles which rise to the surface when it is grubbing about for food amongst the roots of weeds. Angling for Tench is best done in the summer, and very few are caught during the cold months, unless one gets a warm, unseasonable winter's day. Unfortunately, though he puts up a good scrap when hooked, he is covered with slime and handling him is not a pleasant business. Large baits are best for tench, and fishing on the bottom is the most productive, though if the water is not very deep a lightly shotted float can prove successful.

The *Chub* has a reputation for being a very timid fish. It is very easily scared and soon put down by bank or boat noises. It has a preference for fast or medium-flowing waters. It is a sturdy fish with a dark olive back and silvery sides. Pelvic and anal fins are tinted with coral. Because it is a close relative of roach and rudd, it is identified by its *convex* tail fin. It is a greedy feeder and will take almost anything offered, but is a disappointing fighter and after a promising rush, comes in with abject surrender.

When it comes to ferocity and a great provider of sport I favour the *Pike*. He will feed on anything, for not only fish, but frogs, water voles, and even young water fowl form part of his diet. Fierce in his attack, the pike lurks in the weeds, waiting for his prey, and it is not surprising that he is called the freshwater shark. Pike are found in all kinds of waters, canals, ponds, and even fast streams and rivers. He has a long body, a powerful tail, and a snout not unlike that of a crocodile. His teeth slope *backwards*, thereby preventing anything he bites from escaping, and because of this and the fact that his jaws are very strong he needs careful handling when brought to either gaff or landing net. Pike grow to a good size, and as most of his diet is confined to sickly and weak specimens of other fishes, he is a grand fish to have in the waters and wherever there are pike, you will also find that the quality of coarse fish is better.

Last, but not least, amongst the coarse fishes let us mention the *Eel*. This is a first class sporting fish and though the average eel may only weigh about a pound or so, he gives a good fight when hooked. The very tiny, immature bootlace eels are, however, a nuisance and can really tangle your tackle up! But eels are excellent eating, and they take a bait in a sporting manner. Worms make an excellent lure, and eels may be found almost anywhere from dykes to estuaries. In the North, especially in Scotland, eels are regarded with revulsion as 'snake-like' things and, as a northerner it took me a long time to overcome this inbred antipathy. However, I am a convert to eels and eel fishing and have had excellent sport with them in midsummer nights on the English Lakes.

So much for the coarse fishes. As to game fish the *Trout* is the one most likely to be caught. It is to be found in all types of waters ranging from large Scottish lochs to small fast tumbling streams of the West Country. Trout, being game fish, have a different protection season from the fishes I have mentioned earlier, and usually their licence fees are higher. Trout are gallant fighters and bonny to look at. But they do vary in their colourings. A trout taken from a rocky or sandy area will have a rich bluish colour, with red and gold spots, whereas a trout taken from weedy, muddy waters is often yellowish in background hue. In small streams and lakes trout are smallish in size, but in deep lakes and lochs they can attain several pounds weight.

The most popularly accepted method of trout fishing is by fly: wet in lochs and streams in the North, and dry fly in the Southern chalk streams. Worming in fast waters and spinning are also methods used.

The *Sea Trout* is known by several names: finnock, peal, sewin, and herling are its nicknames in different parts of the country. The sea trout is a great fighter and a fresh run fish in from the sea can give you such a battle that your arm will ache from holding the rod. He leaves the water in leaps, dives deep, and generally does everything he can to get off the hook. Sea trout can be fished for in the sea and in estuaries, but they require a special licence.

As for *Salmon*: very few of us ever get the chance to fish for them, and their appearance must be familiar to all. Good salmon fishing costs a lot of money and thousands of pounds are paid every year for the right to fish portions of river, known as 'beats'.

There are other fish to be caught, of course, and amongst the fresh water fishes there are three worth mentioning: the barbel which frequents the weir pools and though completely inedible puts up the most ferocious scrap when hooked, the gudgeon, a tiny relative, only an ounce or so in weight, which can be fished for on delicate tackle, and a species which is only now beginning to become known to British anglers, the zander or pike-perch. These latter fish appear to have a great future and are about to be introduced into our waters: they should attain a weight of up to 30 pounds, but of course their introduction is arousing a lot of controversy.

3　Saltwater Fishes

The number of saltwater fishes is immense: some are fairly commonly captured, others are comparatively rare and cause a minor sensation, sometimes even local newspaper news when caught.

I think it is best to divide the sea fishes likely to be caught into two groups. The first group is known as flat fishes: the second group is known as round fishes.

Flat fishes, ironically enough, do not swim on their stomachs, but actually swim on their sides! The flounder, the plaice, the sole, and the dab are typical flat fishes and their appearance must be well known from the fishmongers' stalls. However, all flat fishes start off in life as round fishes, with one eye on each side of their head. Gradually as they grow they begin to capsize, as it were, and turn on to one side and one eye gradually works through the body and ultimately both eyes appear on the one side of the fish, the upper side. One identifies a flat fish by the position of its eyes as well as by its colours. For instance, fish with eyes on their right side are the flounder, the sole, the dab: fishes with their eyes on the left include the brill and the turbot.

Let us look at the flat fishes first, then. The *Dab,* sometimes called the sand dab, is generally sandy on the upper side and carries a number of brown and orange flecks. The skin is rough on the upper side and the mouth is at the end of the snout. It feeds on the bottom and likes to mouth the bait before taking, so the strike should be light.

The *Flounder* is often found in fresh water, too. The appearance is similar to the dab but the colour is greenish, brownish, or sometimes greyish. The back skin is smooth. There is a special method of fishing for flounders with a baited spoon, a method I will describe later.

The *Plaice* is a bigger fish than either the Dab or the Flounder and can weigh up to 4 pounds. Its general colour is brown and it has a number of very well defined red or orange spots. Behind the eyes, and in a line, there are also a number of hard knobs.

The *Sole* is not very often caught by anglers, and feeds mostly at night, but the *Turbot* which can well turn the scales at over a score of pounds is well sought after. Strong tackle is needed for this fish, which can be identified not only on account of its large size, but by its diamond shape and the dark blotches on its brown back.

The *Brill* is not often caught by shore anglers, but is taken by boatmen: it favours deep water and can weigh anything up to about 14 pounds.

Of the round fishes, probably the best known of all from the sporting standpoint is the *Mackerel*. This is a beautiful fish, and there is no need to describe it. However, it should be eaten as soon as possible after being caught, otherwise it can go 'off' and cause food poisoning. The best known fish after the mackerel, and needing no description, is the *Cod*. This fish can grow to an enormous size, and though codling, from a pound to 4 pounds are usually caught from the shore, large cod of over 20 pounds are not uncommon. Along with the *Whiting*, another member of the cod family, the cod provides good sport round our shores during the winter months. Voracious feeders, they will take almost any bait offered, and if the tackle is not too heavy, make a decent fight.

Amongst sporting sea fishes, the *Bass* must rank high. This fish goes by many names and is also known as the sand bass, sea perch, salmon bass, white salmon. It does, in fact, belong to the perch family and has a spiny dorsal fin. When this is erected it can inflict a painful wound on the hand of the careless fisherman. They are fished for at all times of the year, and range from 'school' bass of but a few ounces to fine specimens of over 10 pounds. As bass are fish with big mouths, they require large baits and big hooks.

The *Pollack* and the *Coalfish* are also other sporting sea fishes: the latter are chiefly found in Scottish waters. They are alike in appearance, and both fishes like to take a moving bait so that spinning and driftlining are successful methods to use. Both fish can also be fished for by the use of flies, and the special fly used for them is known as a 'cuddy' fly. Both fish are game fighters and will try to get to the bottom in a terrific first rush after the bait has been taken: this must be stopped or the battle will be lost in favour of the fish. You see, when they take that first wild plunge to the depths they seek the shelter of the weeds, to which they hang on for dear life. Pulling on the line and trying to reel in will only result in either the hook being torn from the mouth of the fish or the line breaking. The correct procedure is to let the line slacken a little: this lulls the fish into believing that it is safe and so it relaxes in order to move elsewhere; the moment it takes up line to move off, then go into action and by 'pumping' (which I will describe in a later chapter) get that fish towards the landing net.

Finally, amongst the sea fishes in which the angler is likely to take his sport, is the *Mullet* family. There are three members of this family, known as the thick-lipped grey mullet, the golden mullet, and the thin-lipped grey mullet. The red mullet, in spite of its name, belongs to another family of fishes.

The grey mullet is probably the most cunning fish on the list of British saltwater fishes. In fact, if an angler really wishes to test his skill – then the mullet is the fish for him!

Though mullet are anything but easy to catch, they are without any doubt whatever the best fish for the freshwater angler to try for when he takes up sea fishing. Good groundbaiting, careful casting, and the selection of tackle is as essential in mullet fishing as in successful roach hunting.

There are other sea fishes which the angler may go after: for instance, the *Wrasse,* which is found on rocky coastlines, gives good sport, but is worthless from the food point of view. There are *Dogfishes,* a species of small shark which can sometimes be an absolute nuisance, but are good sport on an otherwise blank day: and there are fishes which I shall call *Big Game Fish* and deal with in another Chapter. These include the Sharks, the Skates, and the Conger Eels.

4 Difference between Sea and Freshwater Fishing

So far we have only dealt with angling generally, and listed some of the fishes one is likely to catch in fresh water and in the sea. There seems to the beginner to be a great distinction between sea angling and freshwater angling. In many respects this is true, but basically the differences are not too great. For example, the fundamental tools of angling, common to both branches of the sport, are a rod, a reel, a line, and a hook to which some form of bait or lure is attached. And the principles of using these tools are basically the same, too: though there are slight variations in techniques either for special species sought or for angling conditions.

For example, let's take float fishing. Now this is a method which is most commonly seen in freshwater angling. But float fishing, too, is very important in sea fishing. Floats are used for many purposes: (1) as an indication that a fish is taking the bait, (2) to 'swim' a baited hook into some place where the angler cannot cast his bait (3) to keep the bait at a predetermined depth, or to keep it clear of underwater weeds, or just off the bottom.

Now the basic difference between freshwater fishing and sea fishing (apart from the different size of the fish) is the factor known as the tides.

There are no tides on inland waters, but the sea covers and uncovers stretches of land twice daily. These 'tides' as they are known, flow, that is rise and cover the shore, twice a day: their retreat, or uncovering of the beaches, is known as the ebb. But the tide never ebbs and flows at the same time each day. Tides also vary in height. The highest tides, those with the deepest waters, are known as 'spring' tides, and the low tides are known as 'neap' tides. These occur respectively at fortnightly intervals for highest and lowest period. The 'spring' tides coincide with the full moon and the new moon, and the 'neap' tides at first and last quarter. The gravitational pull of the moon is the cause of the tides. However, these can be predicted to a certain extent, and various tidal forecasts are issued by the Admiralty; they can usually also be bought locally at fishing tackle shops along the coast.

Tides times and heights are only approximate, and here a word of warning. They may rise or fall more or less than the predicted height, and be earlier or later, depending upon meteorological conditions. An off-shore wind can hold a tide back, keep its height down. An on-shore wind can increase its speed and also its height.

This is important because when you go fishing along the coast it is essential to know approximate tide heights and times to prevent yourself being cut off and put into a danger-ous position, if not drowned, as well as putting other folk to inconvenience and danger in trying to rescue you.

Because the tide covers and uncovers the beach, it enables the angler to examine the area in which he will be fishing. He can look at the sea bottom, perhaps even collect his bait there, and also note any obstacles which might cause him to lose his tackle.

This does not happen in inland waters unless there is a drought, or when water is drawn off from a canal or reservoir, thus exposing the bed of the fishing ground. But whereas the sea fish move out with the ebbing tide, and come in again on the flow to feed, when inland waters are reduced by drought or draining off, the poor fish left behind are stranded and often die for lack of oxygen in the water. This usually entails major rescue operations in damming up small sections of river, or removing the fish to other waters.

Except for heavy rainfalls causing floods or spates in rivers and streams, most waters are fairly constant in inland fishing. They may be described as still waters, such as lakes, reservoirs, canals or slow-moving streams or rivers, or fast-moving waters. But each day the sea experiences all phenomena. When the tide is at its height, or at its lowest, there occurs what is known as a 'stand', that is, the waters remain still, but during the ebbing and flowing there is a fast current and a

26

decreasing one, so that when fishing throughout a tide the sea angler can experience the sensations of still water, slow-moving waters, and fast waters, in both directions: something the freshwater angler may have to visit several waters to experience.

This does affect, not the basic elements of fishing tackle, but in float fishing the size of the float. Where waters are still, the float may be as light and as small as possible, having regard to the weight of the baited hook: but the faster and rougher the water and the heavier the bait, the larger the float must be. That is why you will see such slender floats used in canal fishing, and such large floats used by the saltwater angler.

One other basic difference between saltwater fishing and freshwater fishing is the depth of water: apart from some of the Scottish and Irish lochs and loughs and the English lakes, most freshwater fishing grounds are comparatively shallow – even 20 feet being considered quite deep. For some species of fish, such as char, fished for in Lake Windermere, for example, great depths are encountered. But when sea fishing, especially from a boat off-shore, depths of 50 or 60 fathoms (and each fathom is 6 feet) are nothing unusual. The average saltwater fish, too, runs to a larger size, and currents in the sea run very strongly. So strong, in fact, that whereas a 2-ounce weight is considered heavy in freshwater fishing, weights of over 2 pounds are often required to get a sea line down to the bottom and hold it there against the pull of the current against the line.

No one can say which is the better form of angling – some anglers like the call of the sea – others prefer the quiet of some canal or stream – so one cannot say one form of angling is better than another. That is a basic truth.

Because some fishermen who take part in freshwater fishing competitions have specialised in using ultra-fine tackle and catching very tiny fish, usually bleak, some folk term freshwater angling as 'tiddler-snatching': on the other hand because sea fishing sometimes demands extra strong rods and lines of 40 to 50 pounds breaking strain with weights of up to 2 pounds, some anglers sneer at saltwater men and talk about them fishing with cables and telegraph poles. Both these critics are ignorant and biased – and the truth lies elsewhere. One can fish with strong tackle for pike and carp in British freshwater, and strong tackle is used for salmon fishing: for the smelt and the mullet and the mackerel, light tackle, comparable with freshwater equipment is used. There is only one thing to bear in mind – the basic difference is that whereas you can use your equipment in both sea fishing and freshwater fishing, salt water is very corrosive and greater care must be taken to clean your equipment after use.

Basically, the techniques of angling, with few exceptions which I describe in the next chapter, are common to both types of fishing: and where there are differences I will tell you about them in connection with separate species, or angling conditions.

Today, for the first time in British angling history, there is a great interchange of anglers who take part in both sea fishing and freshwater fishing, and they get great fun and enjoyment from both branches.

5 Types of Fishing Tackle

I have said earlier that the basic requirements of angling are a rod, a reel, a line, and a hook with some form of bait or lure. There are, of course, additional items which the angler will require, and these are floats, leads or weights to take the baited hook down to the right depth (hence the expression 'hook, line and sinker') and different types of baits. Baits, even artificial ones, I will not include under the heading of tackle, but will deal with each of these in separate chapters.

The rod

Rods used to be made of many different materials: cane, split cane, Spanish reed, greenheart, steel, and lastly glass fibre. But today, the trend is definitely in favour of glass fibre, and these are usually of two types, hollow (i.e. tubular rods) or solid. Sometimes you get a combination of the two, a solid bottom piece or butt, and a hollow tip. Quite candidly, after many years of experience, I would now only plump for glass fibre rods: they have their faults and limitations, but, believe me, anglers themselves have greater faults and limitations!

The rod consists of three main components: butt, centre section, tip. The butt is the part which is held by the angler and is generally covered with cork, though sometimes, especially in sea rods, can be of polished wood.

The centre section is, as may be imagined, the central portion of the rod. The action of the rod is going to be concentrated in the tip, where the greatest bend is, and where the rod section is finest. There is, especially in sea rods where big fish are encountered, considerable action, too, in the centre section, but in general the butt and centre sections are not going to bend: in the case of the centre section this is not entirely true, because some action will take place in it.

Rods may also be described as two or three piece. This merely refers to the number of sections which make up a rod. Thus the normal rod consists of sections which are fitted together by means of ferrules. These are slightly tapered and a little grease helps to keep it easy to pull the rod apart at the end of the day. When the rod is put together the rings through which the line must pass must be all in the same line. Simple enough, but quite often the beginner forgets this.

The rings I have referred to guide the fishing line along the rod and are so spaced that they follow its curve without putting any strain on either rings or line. The two most important rings are the end or top ring, and the ring nearest to the butt. These are generally made from different materials: some are stainless steel, others have liners of porcelain or agatine. It is best to have all the rings of one material, and in my opinion stainless steel rings throughout are preferable.

Here there is a slight difference between freshwater rods and saltwater rods. A lot of freshwater fishing depends upon a quick 'tip action'. This means that the rod has to be fairly stiff so that the tip reacts quickly to a sudden strike by the fisherman. This type of rod is usually fairly lengthy. On the other hand, a rod which is designed for 'legering' (I will describe this method later) is usually shorter and the action travels through the rod down to the butt. And this brings us to the fascinating subject of test curves.

What is a test curve? Well, take your rod and fasten it so that it stands upright. Now pull the rod tip over until the angle between the rod top joint and the butt is at right angles (90°). This may be found out by loading it with lead weights or by pulling against a spring balance. The figure shown will be the pounds pressure required to do this. Thus, if it takes 16 pounds to pull the rod to this position, the test curve loading would be 16 pounds.

Now, divide the test curve loading you have found (e.g. 2 pounds) by 16 and this will give you the ideal weight which the rod should cast. For a 2-pound test curve rod, a weight of 2 ounces would be fine. From this it is fairly simple to find the best weight of line to use with the rod: simply multiply the test curve by five. And in the instance given, this could be up to 10 pounds line. Simple, isn't it?

So far we have talked about the basic essential of a rod. But there's more to it than that. There is no such thing as a *general* rod – anyone who tries to sell you a rod for general fishing is simply kidding you. Just imagine how impossible such a rod would really be: light enough in tip action for match fishing, stout enough to cast heavy leger weights, supple enough for trolling and spinning, balanced enough for fly fishing, and able to tackle anything from a bleak of an ounce or so to a salmon or pike of 30 pounds!

No – there are specialist rods for specialist jobs. Let's face it, even the common or garden pencil varies according to its shape, and hardness or softness of the lead. Rods may be grouped into the following main headings:

Freshwater rods :	Match fishing and competition
	legering
	spinning
	fly fishing
	bait casting
Saltwater rods :	Pier and boat fishing
	light spinning rods
	big game rods
	beach casting rods

Again, the rods will vary according to the size of the fish being sought. So, when selecting your first rod, try to find out first of all where you are going to fish and the type of fish you are likely to catch. You have probably got some friends who already go fishing in the area, and they'll be able to tell you all about it. But in any case don't take their words as Gospel true because they may be fishing wrongly, though right about the fish you are likely to catch. Go along and watch people fishing there, see the way they go about it, look at their rods, but don't make a nuisance of yourself and bother them when they are actually trying to land a fish or just casting. Wait for a lull in the sport: they won't mind answering your questions if you put them politely.

The advice I always give to adults who try out a sport is this and this applies to all sports: don't go all out and buy expensive equipment first time out. I have known people take up ice-skating, go mad about it, and on their second visit to a rink purchase boots, skates, the lot, and a few weeks later give it up. The same thing happens with other sports and games. No, what I suggest is that you try to let a friend or a relative loan you his tackle and go with you to test it out. If you really want to fish you'll be content to do this first of all. Then, when you are quite sure you are going to continue – think about purchasing the tackle. Rods are not cheap, they can score up to £15 and more: so I would suggest you try to get a cheapish rod to start with and then, if you don't want to carry on, you won't have lost too much valuable pocket money.

Of course, birthdays and Christmases are all very well, one can drop hints to parents as to what is required, but the fishing urge generally starts when the coarse fishing season opens in June: and if you have to save up to buy a rod, perhaps doing a paper round, remember the cold, miserable, dark winter's mornings you have had to go through to achieve your ambition. So be wise – don't commit yourself until you are certain you *are* going to continue angling.

When you are certain – then go all out and buy the best you can afford, because this will be the cheapest in the long run.

I illustrate here some butts which show the different types of rod: both bottom rods and spinning rods often have similar butts: fly rods have the reel fitting at the very bottom, whilst bait casting rods have what is known as an off-set handle. Special long rods for salmon fishing, and beach casting rods for sea anglers who have to try to cast a line at least 100 to 150 yards have long butts and are known as two-handed action rods: otherwise rods only use one hand for casting purposes.

With all this in mind, and having visited the spot where you wish to fish, go along to your local tackle dealer: and if there are two or three in a district, go to the one who is always ready to deal with youngsters. Most shops will give you a fair deal, recognising that the young angler who is properly treated will become a permanent and much more lucrative customer when he is an adult. Don't be afraid to tell the sales-

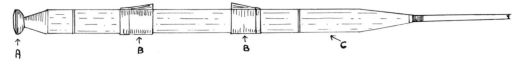

Figure 2 Butt or handle of a typical rod. (A) rod button; (B) reel or winch fitting; (C) Cork covered handle. This is typical of both spinning and bottom rods.

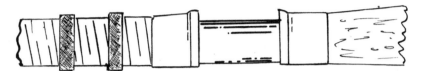

Figure 3 A Screw-winch fitting.

Figure 4 Butt of a typical fly rod. Note the reel fitting below the cork hand grip.

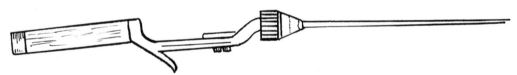

Figure 5 Offset handle of a bait-casting rod. A multiplier or close-faced reels are generally used with these rods.

man how much you wish to spend, and where you are going to fish. He'll respect your confidence and try to help you. If the shopkeeper doesn't want to be bothered, or tries to sell you something rather offhandedly, find another shop. If more anglers followed this advice there would be fewer disappointments at the waterside.

But, when telling the salesman what you wish to spend,

don't forget that this has to include the price of the reel, the cost of the line, and some hooks and other items as well. It's no good spending everything on a rod and then having to put a stupid cheap reel on it.

The reel

Though the rod and reel are two separate pieces of equipment, the angler cannot consider one without the other. A rod and a reel must balance: to take matters to extremes think how idiotic it would be to fix a heavy big game fish reel to a lightweight match rod! The two must be in harmony and no rod should be bought nor reel purchased until the reel has been placed on the rod, the rod assembled and the whole outfit tested for balance. Perhaps it would be more correct to state, test for 'feel'. If the outfit feels right, then it must be right. The balance may be varied a little according to the personal taste of the angler and most butts are fitted with winch or reel fittings which allow its position to be varied.

Irrespective of the type of fishing to be done, in the sea or in freshwater, reels are grouped into main types:

(1) Centre-pin reels
(2) Fixed-spool models
(3) Multipliers, and a cross between (1) and (2)
(4) Side-casters

The centre-pin reel consists of a drum which revolves on an axle. In order to wind the line in after it has been cast out there are generally two handles on one side of the drum: it also usually, though not always in cheap models, incorporates a ratchet device. The drum may consist of a number of materials, wood, plastic, steel, aluminium. There are today a lot of very large diameter centre-pin reels, known as Scarborough Reels, in use by sea anglers, and often these have a diameter of 8 or more inches. The centre-pin reel was the first of the fishing reels and is still popular today. Some match anglers like to use them with large drums but narrow in the flange: these factors enable them to recover the line quickly. For some angling methods, such as allowing a float

34

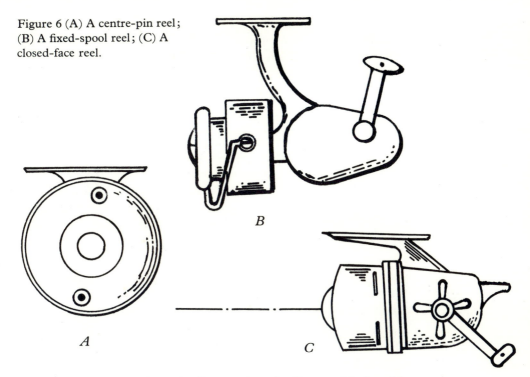

Figure 6 (A) A centre-pin reel;
(B) A fixed-spool reel; (C) A
closed-face reel.

B

A

C

to run downsteam ('trotting') carrying the line and bait with
it, a centre-pin is ideal.

Fixed-spool reels are probably in more use today, especially by freshwater anglers, than any other reel. They make
casting easy. The line comes off the spool at right angles and
is picked up and replaced on the reel by a moving pick-up or
bale arm when the handle is turned to recover the line.

The great majority of fixed-spool reels have what is termed
a 'slipping clutch' built into their mechanism. This acts as a
safety factor should a fish make a sudden rush when being
held, and this stops the line from breaking. The great advantage which the fixed-spool reel has over the centre-pin is that
one may carry two or three spare spools with different breaking strains of line on them. This enables the fisherman to
change line strengths in but a fraction of the time it would
take to wind off and rewind another line on to a centre-pin
reel.

The term 'fixed' might be wrong, because though the

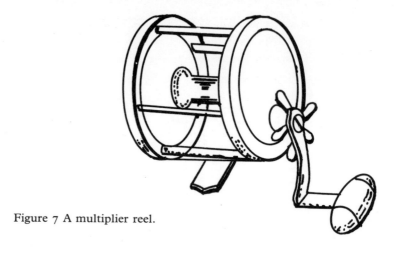

Figure 7 A multiplier reel.

spool does not revolve, it does in fact move backwards and forwards whilst line is being picked up and laid on it. This ensures uniformity of line over the spool surface.

There are two types of fixed-spool reel, the open reel and the closed-face reel. This latter is generally used with bait casting rods and is operated by a lever at the rear of the reel. Unlike centre-pin and fixed-spool reels which are normally operated beneath the rod, the closed-face reel and also the multiplier are used on top of the rod.

The multiplier reel, as its name suggests, derives its name from the fact that its spool or drum revolves via a system of gears at a speed greater than that of the recovery handle. It is also equipped with a device which lays the line evenly along the drum. The multiplier reel is very popular with sea anglers as it enables them to cast enormous distances, and is very suitable for use with heavy baits or weights. There is the great drawback to the multiplier reel that it is rather a complicated mechanism, and therefore expensive to purchase, and also the time taken to learn to use it properly is much longer than with any other type of reel.

However, if the angler first learns on a centre-pin reel and learns to control the flight of the bait through the air by using thumb or forefinger pressure against the rim of the reel, he can apply the same technique to the multiplier.

The side-caster reel combines the best of both worlds of centre-pin and fixed-spool. The spool is turned sideways so that it may be used like a fixed spool reel for casting, but for line recovery it is turned to centre-pin position.

Fly fishing reels are based on the centre-pin principle, though some modern models have automatic recovery devices built into them.

The line

Once upon a fishing time there were many varieties of line and casts to consider, flax, cutty-hunk, cotton, silk, catgut, and so on. Today the choice is invariably nylon. This does not rot or fray, as the old lines did, and comes ready for the angler in many different sizes and breaking strains on plastic spools which are easy to wind on to the reel. Breaking strains should be given wet and dry, and it is the wet breaking strain which is important. One disadvantage of nylon is that it has great elasticity, and the line stretch can, especially if sea fishing with strong line, result in a collapsed spool owing to the strain it places on it. When long lengths of line are out, the elasticity does prevent the angler keeping in close touch with the fish and can affect the efficiency of his strike.

There are two main types of nylon line, monofilament and braided. The braided lines are best for sea fishing, and should be used when a multiplier reel is employed.

Hooks

These are terribly important. A blunt, bent, rusty, or weakened hook can lose a fish quicker than anything. Hooks must be selected with care: the temper must be right so it's no use buying cheap hooks. All hooks are sold by number size, and the higher the number the smaller the hook. Thus a size 12 would be a smaller hook than a size 6. This is based on what is known as the 'Redditch' scale. And just as there are many variations in floats and other items of tackle, hooks vary tremendously in their shapes and bends. For most freshwater fishing, the 'Crystal' bend hook is the best, or the 'Model

Perfect'. The sea angler will occasionally use very big hooks especially if after shark, tope, or large fish, and these often have a swivel and a wire trace incorporated into their construction.

Hooks are also distinguished by their ends. These may be termed 'eyed', in which the hook shank terminates in a small eye through which the line is fastened: spade-ended, in which the shank is flattened: or straight-shanked to which the line is whipped and held by some form of adhesive. For the beginner I would strongly suggest that he buys hooks 'to gut' or 'to nylon' – this means that the hooks are already attached to an appropriate length of nylon for the size of the hook: this saves the trouble of trying to tie hooks to the trace at the waterside, and anything which makes angling simpler in the beginning is well worth while.

The hook, the line, the reel, and the rod are the basic elements: with variations in length and weight for different purposes, the young angler must not select a rod which is too long for him to handle in comfort: nor should he buy any of those silly little 3-foot jobs sold in some shops as 'boy's rods'. They are nothing of the kind, and a waste of the young angler's money.

In addition to the basic items we have now to consider what specific items of tackle should be used for different angling tasks: these include things like floats, leads, and other tackle.

6   Floats, Leads, and other things

As I have said earlier, floats may be used for many different purposes. They are also manufactured from a great many different materials. In fact, they can be made so exciting and attractive from the eager angler's point of view that it is difficult not to start making a collection of them.

When choosing the float the angler has to ask himself two questions. Firstly, what type of water am I going to fish, is it still, fast-moving, or will it vary in depth? Secondly, he has to think about the weight of the hook and bait it has to carry, and the weight and strength of the line to be used.

Still waters require light small floats, but in fast-moving waters a lot of weight may be required to get the bait near the bottom, and this means that the float must be much bigger. Sometimes a float may be ideal in still waters if it just balances the weight of the baited hook. The answer is to use the lightest, smallest float you can compatible with conditions in hand, i.e. wind strength, depth of water, fish sought and so on.

Floats should possess a most distinctive colour on the top, so that the angler may see them at once. Fluorescent paints are ideal for this. But the underside must appear to fish as something which is naturally upon the water: white, dark green, or dark brown are popular colours for this.

Sea floats are generally large, and made of cork, though I have encountered celluloid and plastic models. But freshwater floats may consist of many different materials. Celluloid floats are popular. They are cheap to buy, they are light to carry and they can be loaded well with shot. They are waterproof and can easily be kept clean. Floats may also be made from 'quills' either from crows, geese, turkeys, or porcupines. They are mainly used for 'light' angling and vary in length from 4 to 10 inches in length.

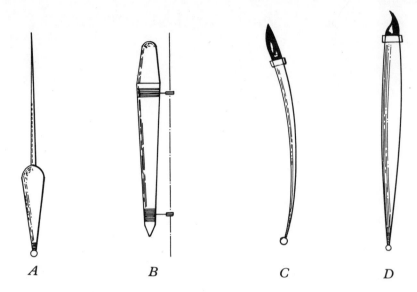

A   B   C   D

Figure 8 A selection of floats. (A) Antenna float; (B) Sliding float; (C) A crow quill float; (D) A porcupine quill float.

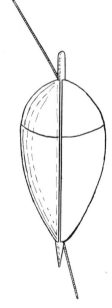

Figure 9 A cork-bodied sea angling float.

Special mention should be made of the antenna type of float. This model has a long, slender antenna extending from the top. This offers very little wind resistance and is very suitable for use on windy days when the water surface is rough. The float should be loaded so that only the antenna shows.

Another type of float is the self-cocking variety in which the lead shot is carried inside the body of the float.

Sea anglers use a special float known as a sliding-float. This is used for fishing deep water and is free to ride up and down the line. It usually has rings attached to its centre and end through which the line may run freely. When placed on the line it drops immediately to the lead or hook. To use it the angler predetermines the depth at which it is to be used and at that point on the line attaches a piece of rubber tubing, thin enough to slip easily through the rod rings, but thick enough to prevent it being dragged through the float rings. When the tackle is used the float slides up to the rubber stop, but when

40

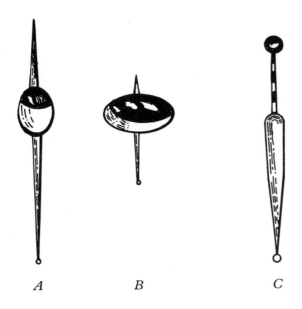

Figure 10 Another selection of floats. (A) A cork and quill float; (B) A
sea float; (C) A beacon antenna float.

reeling in the angler can retrieve all his line as the float slips
back towards the hook. This is very vital for deep water
fishing, for if an ordinary float were used attached to the line,
and the angler had, say, 20 feet between hook and float, he
would be in rather a difficult position trying to bring in a
hooked fish because when the standard float jammed against
the top ring he would not be able to retrieve any more line and
the fish would still be in a fair depth of water.

Most cork floats used for sea fishing have a hole drilled
vertically through the centre into which a wooden plug is
inserted. Some have a slit cut into the side meeting the central
hole so that it is easy to add or remove a float at any time.

Leads

These take many forms and sizes. They are required to get
the bait into the proper position and may be used with float
fishing, or in leger fishing to keep the bait on the bottom.

41

Figure 11 Two typical sea leads. (A)
Watch lead and (B) torpedo lead, are
both used on sandy bottoms.

A   B

In freshwater fishing with the float split shots made from
lead are the usual form and these range in sizes from what is
termed 'dust' shot to 'swan' shot. In addition there are small
flat fold-over leads which may be fastened to the line, and
lead wire which can be wrapped round the line. Split shots are
fixed to the line or trace by pinching them together.

For legering, where the bait is kept on the bottom, there
are many different shapes of leads ranging from drilled
spherical balls to box-shaped leads (through which a central
hole has been drilled) known as 'coffin leads', and stream-
lined peardrop leads, some with swivels, some without,
known as bombs, and triangular leads of which the swivelled
'Capta' is the best known.

Sea anglers also use a variety of leads known as grip and
watch leads, lighthouse leads, all of which are illustrated here.
Owing to the strength of tides, and the varying nature of the
sea bed these must stand up to the scouring motion of the
sea, yet not get caught up in patches of weed or rock, nor sink
so deeply into the mud that they hide the bait.

Other items

It is necessary for the angler to have a landing net. This
usually has a metal frame and can be folded up to put away. A
landing net should *always* be ready for use when the angler is

fishing because he never knows the moment when he is going to need it. The best material for landing nets is nylon, as it is easy to wash and keep clean.

A disgorger is necessary. This is used for taking the hook out of the mouth of a fish without either injuring the fish or breaking the line. In addition, if the angler is going pike fishing, or after sea fish, a pike gag is another useful item. It holds the jaws of the fish open whilst the hook is extracted, though care is needed as a strong pike can close his jaws on even a stout gag.

Other items necessary are a bait can for live bait, boxes in which hooks, casts, and so on can be kept, and boxes in which bait is kept. A stout knife, preferably with a cork handle so that it will float if dropped into the water, and a pair of good waterproof boots complete the beginner's outfit.

7   Angling Techniques – Casting

Before learning about the different techniques of angling, float fishing, bottom fishing, spinning, fly fishing, and so on, the beginner should learn how to cast. This merely means knowing how to throw the line with the hook, or lure, or float, with accuracy into the required spot.

Thus it may only be necessary to gently swing a lightly loaded float tackle a few feet into a quiet pool; on the other hand it may be necessary to 'aim' the tackle to land under overhanging bushes on the other side of a stream into the dimples of a rising fish, or beyond a hidden obstacle such as underwater rocks, or to some selected spot upstream so that the bait may be drifted naturally over unsuspicious fish.

Does this sound like a tall order?

First of all the method of casting depends upon the type of equipment being used. Shall we start with the centre-pin reel first?

Centre-pin reel techniques

First of all, stand facing the point at which you are going to cast. Then strip off a little line with the left hand (I am here assuming you are holding the rod in the right hand) then gently swing the rod tip back and forward and let the stripped-off line shoot out. Keep doing this, recovering the line with the left hand and stripping off a little from the reel each time, until you can gently drop the baited hook into the target area. A good method to practise is with an inflatable rubber ring on a pond, or even on the lawn.

For longer casts, where more weight is needed, the line may be cast direct from the reel. Here the movement is from backward to forward, with an overhead motion, the baited

44

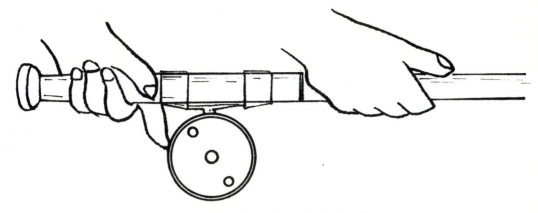

Figure 12 This shows how the forefinger is used as a brake on the rim of a centre-pin reel when casting.

hook and weight being suspended from the tip of the rod at the rear, then the rod is gently swung forward with an accelerating motion and as the line straightens and starts to shoot through the rings it is watched until it begins to fall; the forefinger or thumb is then gently applied to the rim of the reel in a braking motion, to prevent overruns and the consequent tangle the line would get into, known as a bird's nest.

Fixed spool reel

This is easily learned. Hold the rod handle with the leg or foot of the reel between the second and third fingers. Trap the line against the rod handle with the forefinger. Now drop the pick-up or bale arm so that the line is left free for casting. It is only the pressure of your forefinger against the line holding it against the rod handle which prevents it spilling off the reel.

Now, look at the point where you are going to place the bait. Point the rod directly at it, then bring it back in a sharp sweep to the direct overhead position. This is done by using only the wrist, *not* the arm. Without pausing bring the rod forward again with pressure of wrist and thumb and the moment the rod reaches the 10 o'clock position, lift the forefinger and release the line. The line will peel off the spool and should fly straight towards the selected point.

Should the cast have been too powerful, or if you wish to stop the lure before it hits the water, just trap the line again with the forefinger. If done properly the cast will have been beautifully made. However, the beginner often finds that the lure either lands at his feet or flies vertically into the air. This is due to holding on too long with the forefinger.

As soon as the bait hits the water and the slack line has been reeled in the rod tip should be lowered to a horizontal position.

The multiplier

This is a different proposition altogether. Whereas the fore-finger has been used to control the line with the fixed spool reel, now it is the thumb which becomes important. In fact, the key to good casting with the multiplier reel is correct thumb control.

Again, first of all point the rod towards the target, and with the thumb of the casting hand resting on the reel and pressing *lightly* against the line and spool flange raise the rod backward and overhead to the 2 o'clock position. Now quickly check the rod and snap the wrist forward and *downward*. At the same time that the rod comes back to the upright position release the thumb pressure on the line to allow the bait to shoot forward. Continue dropping the rod until the 9 o'clock position is reached and watch, all the time, the flight of the lure to the target. Apply thumb pressure slowly to reduce its speed and as it reaches the target stop the drum spool by thumb pressure.

The backward and forward movement of the rod must be made smoothly and without any noticeable pause or jerk.

Finally, having cast the line, there is the question of its recovery.

Recovery of line

With a centre-pin line this is simplicity itself. The line is recovered by turning on the handles but with the fixed-spool reel, with the slipping-clutch involved, there are other facts to think about.

46

Whatever the temptation might be, if you have hooked a fish on a fixed-spool reel, never wind in against the slipping clutch when playing a fish. If you do so you will kink the line terribly, and may even cause it to break.

The multiplier, of course, recovers at a much faster rate than the turning of the handle and presents few difficulties in this respect.

But freshwater and sea anglers alike must guard against casting too far. It is the practice today to look upon long distance casting as something to be emulated. Sea anglers using the 'lay back' method cast enormous distances – but very often short casts find fish feeding within a few yards of the angler. In point of fact one can over-cast. It is nice to know that one cast may reach a record distance, but feeling the fish take at that distance is another matter!

Just think about it – whereas you may cast across a wide river to catch fish within a foot of the opposite bank, the angler on the other side can be doing the same. Both of you are being idiots and discourteous to each other.

When playing a hooked fish there is often a mistake made in keeping the rod too near the vertical. 'Keep your rod tip up!' How often is that shouted to some newcomer. This is all right up to a point, but 'up' should not mean vertical, certainly no more than 60°, otherwise the strain of the battle will be thrown against the top and centre joints and can well result in a damaged rod. When recovering the line by 'pumping', that is by dropping the rod tip and then reeling in the slack, the rod should only be dropped to about 30°, otherwise too much strain will be brought upon the line itself, and of course the reel and the action of the rod wasted.

Above all, though a fish must be held, he must not be held too hard, especially in the case of a fixed-spool outfit, or he will be lost.

Except for very small fishes, they should not be lifted from the water and wound in to hand. The function of a rod and reel is to cast a line and recover it – it has not been designed as a crane and weight-lifting is not part of its function. The landing net and the gaff are the instruments for bringing the fish to basket.

Angling Techniques – Float Fishing

This is a very popular method and probably used by more anglers than any other.

First of all the depth of the water is found out by plumbing. To do this you use a conically-shaped lead weight which has a piece of cork in the base. These are generally bought in $\frac{1}{2}$-ounce or 1-ounce sizes for freshwater fishing. The top of the plummet has a ring attached and the hook is put through this and carried down the lead and the point of the hook pushed into the cork base. Now, gently lower the plummet from the rod tip until the bottom is found. When the plummet is resting on the bottom and the line is taut the tip of the float should be level with the surface.

Now, having selected the right float and baited it, balance it with enough lead shot, or sinkers, so that the slightest touch of the bait by an interested fish will cause it to sink. The best way to do this is to place the weights near the float and this allows the baited hook to sink in a natural manner. When the cast has been made the line must be adjusted so that the float is nicely cocked and balanced.

When the float dips, the angler strikes: or if it suddenly lies flat on the surface, or begins to move about, a strike is made. But what is striking? It is merely the response of the angler to the float movement, the rod is lifted sufficiently to lift the float and this should set the hook point correctly in the mouth of the fish. Too weak a strike and the fish is away, scared: too strong or vigorous a strike and the line or the rod tip itself can break, or the fish, if small enough can be pulled straight out of the water like an arrow from a bow and go straight back over the angler's head! Don't laugh. I have seen this happen.

The freshwater man has several terms for float fishing. One of them is 'trotting' – I think this is self-explanatory. It is practised on fast-flowing waters, and the angler casts the float out slightly upstream and by the time it passes the angler's position the bait should be travelling downstream slightly ahead of the float. Sea anglers often use this method to let the float search out eddies and currents amongst rocks, in order to get to their fish and it is a very good method of wrasse fishing.

'Stret Pegging' is a most peculiar term – in this method the float tackle is allowed to swim downstream, but it is held so that the float is stationary with the bait just waving off the bottom.

'Laying On' also sounds odd until one realises that it means that the bait is anchored to the bottom. This is a combination of float fishing and legering, in that a heavy weight is used to keep the bait in position.

Float fishing in weedy waters can present quite a problem

Figure 13 (Left) FLOAT FISHING (A) Running line; (B) Float; (C) Split shot; (D) Hook. (Right LAYING ON FLOAT FISHING (A) Hook; (B) Shot; (C) Line; (D) Float.

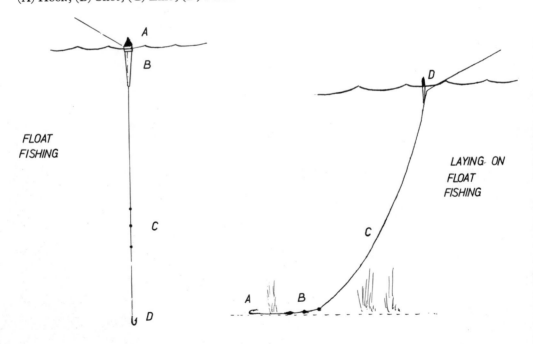

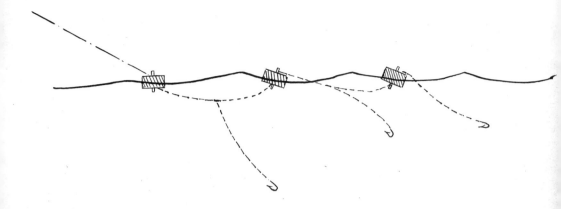

SURFACE TROT FOR MULLET

Figure 14 Surface Trot used for Mullet fishing.

and the chief of these is finding the depth of water between the weeds and the surface. Obviously one cannot use a plummet in the ordinary way to find the depth because it would go straight through the weeds. But if a properly shotted float is used tackle can be set up which will rest the baited hook lightly on top of the weeds.

Set the tackle up normally but put three split shot on the trace about 9 inches apart – the lowest one about 6 inches above the hook. After trying to estimate the depth cast to the desired spot. If the float lies flat on the surface it means that it was set too high up the line and the shotted line is lying on the bottom. So one has to keep casting and retrieving until finally the float lies half-cocked. When this is reached it means that the hook and the lowest split shot are lying on the bottom or on top of the weeds. If the float sits perfectly upright, then shots and hook are clear of the bottom.

Sea anglers, especially when after mullet, use surface trots. This is a form of float fishing which can only be used in calm water, principally harbours. The tackle consists of one or more small cork floats linked together with short lengths of trace between them, from each of which hangs a baited hook.

Plate 2 (*opposite*) Float fishing in still waters.

51

The length of the trace should never drop lower than 1 foot below the floats and the tackle is cast upstream of the mullet and trotted down to them.

9 Angling techniques – Bottom Fishing

Bottom fishing refers to methods in which the bait is allowed to lie naturally on the bottom of the water, but in which no float tackle is involved as in 'laying-on'. The term ground fishing is also used by sea anglers to describe this method.

The favourite method of bottom fishing is that of legering, closely followed by what is termed 'paternostering'. Legering, sometimes also spelt 'ledgering', is very effective in all types of waters, salt and fresh, still and fast running.

Briefly, the leger consists of a running line, the portion of cast or trace on which the leger weight is fixed, and the hook. Though many anglers slide the leger weight on to the cast itself, I consider it much sounder practice to use a short length of fine wire instead. As the leger weight moves up and down the cast it obviously weakens it, especially if fishing over sand, gravel, or rocky bottoms.

To make up the leger, attach the hook-line to about 18 inches to 24 inches of fine wire and just above the hook line pinch on a small split shot, or a piece of lead wire. The purpose of this is to act as a stop, and prevent the leger weight from sliding down on to the baited hook. However, instead of a split shot, a small swivel may be used instead. Now, thread the wire through the hole in the leger body or swivel attachment, according to the type of leger weight used, and then attach the wire to the running line.

As in the case of floats, angling conditions will decide the size of leger weight to use and obviously the faster the water the greater the weight required.

The purpose of the leger rig is to allow a fish to pick up the bait without feeling the weight of the lead. When the bait is taken the fish will draw the wire through the leger and this is signalled to the angler by the rod tip. If the leger weight is too

53

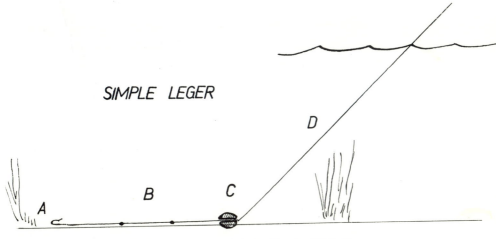

SIMPLE LEGER

A   B   C   D

Figure 15 SIMPLE LEGER in which (A) is baited hook; (B) Split shot or swivel; (C) Leger weight and (D) Line.

heavy the fish may feel its drag and promptly let go the bait. On the other hand if a fish takes the bait and swims upwards with it, the leger weight must not be so light that it would lift off the bottom without drawing the wire through it.

Having cast out the leger rig the angler should then reel in until the line is tight. With most forms of angling it is best to keep the rod in hand so that the strike may be made quickly, but in legering it is best to lay the rod down, using a special rod rest which may vary from a simple stick with a vee-shaped head to an expensive or complicated cradle. Sea anglers fishing from piers and promenades may of course lay their rods against bollards or railings. If shore fishing a good rest can be made from three canes, built up in pyramid fashion with their bases stuck into the sand or shingle and the tops lightly lashed together about 6 inches from the tips so that they cross and form a suitable cradle.

As there is no float to indicate to the angler when a fish is interested, other signal systems have to be used. One method is to keep the line tight and watch the rod tip, any trembling or plucking of the tip usually indicating a bite. Sea anglers, of course, have to contend very often with marauding crabs which give rod tip signals this way, and both sea anglers and

Plate 3 (*opposite*) The author (right) instructs a young friend in casting a sea leger from a centre-pin reel.

river fishermen have occasionally to contend with under-water rubbish which brushes against the line and signals a 'bite'. Another method is to keep the hand on the rod, but have the line laid over the back of the fingers. This indicates when bites are being made, but, unless bites are very frequent, can become tiresome.

Freshwater anglers use a blob of paste, about the size of a damson, on the running line between reel and bottom ring: when this jumps about it is an indication that one should strike. A piece of paper, folded over the line, can also be used. Sea anglers often attach a bell to the rod tip, but as gusts of wind can cause the bell to ring, this is not a very reliable method to use.

One often finds rods specially designed for legering. This type of rod does not require as a rule to be much longer than 8 feet, whereas a float rod, especially a match fishing rod should be from 11 to 15 feet in length. The leger rod is also more stoutly built than the float rod and has a much higher test curve rating.

It's an odd thing, but when one receives instruction on angling it is stressed time and time again, and must go on being stressed, that movement about the waterside must be quiet and cautious. Clothing should not clash with the back-ground. There must be no stamping about on the bank or pier – but when the leger is cast out it drops into the water with a resounding splash! This is, of course, unavoidable, but as the weight immediately sinks to the bottom, it does not seem to have any adverse effect on the fish.

As legering enables the angler to cast further than with a float, there would seem to be greater difficulty in getting ground bait out to where the baited hook is lying. This can be done in several ways. Ground-bait can be mixed up with clay or mud and thrown to the area: it may be squeezed round the leger weight itself: it can be formed round a matchstick which is twisted into the line just above the leger: or one can use a swim-feeder. This usually consists of a hollow cylinder which is free to move up and down the line, filled with bait. The sea angler can also use a similar method, not for groundbaiting but for 'scenting' the area. This is done by using a long cylinder, such as a cigar case, filled with cotton wool which is thoroughly saturated with pilchard or halibut oil. It is attached to the running line by two loops and allowed to run down to the leger. The pilchard, or other sea fish oil, oozes out into the fishing area and helps attract fish there and thence to the bait. It also attracts crabs!

The rolling or roving leger is a good method of fishing. Here, fishing in moving waters, the leger weight is lighter than needed to hold the bottom, and the baited hook and leger is carried along by the current. This enables one to fish a whole area where food would naturally travel to the fish.

The paternoster

This is generally used by freshwater anglers who are after pike and perch, but is commonly used by sea anglers for bottom fishing, and for fishing from boats at varying depths.

The tackle consists basically of a trace about 30 inches long with two or more short traces attached to it to which hooks are attached. The lead weight is at the bottom of the trace so that all the hooks are above it. Individual hook traces should be

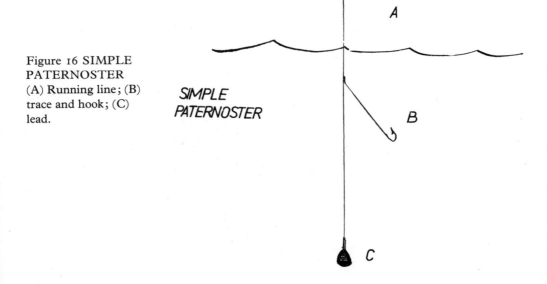

Figure 16 SIMPLE PATERNOSTER (A) Running line; (B) trace and hook; (C) lead.

SIMPLE PATERNOSTER

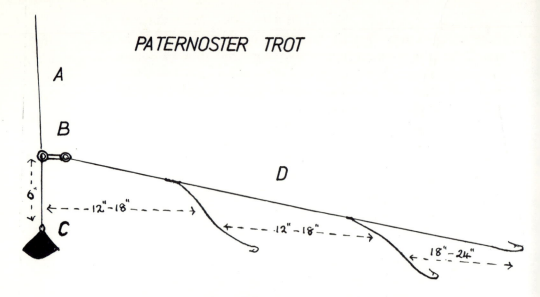

Figure 17 PATERNOSTER TROT used in sea angling. (A) line;
(B) swivel; (C) lead; (D) trace with hooks on at intervals of 1 foot to
18 inches.

from 6 inches to a foot in length. The distance from lead to the
lowest hook should be from 18 inches to 24 inches, according
to the nature of the water bottom. If it is very weedy or very
muddy, then the distance from weight to lowest hook may be
as much as 4 feet in order to keep the bait above the weed or
prevent it sinking into the soft mud and disappearing altogether.

Paternostering is best done from a boat or jetty or some
promontory, as the bait can be swung gently into position,
or just lowered into the water. When fishing from the bank of
a river or lake, a long cast means that the hooks are often too
near the bottom, and may even rest in the weeds. When pike
fishing it is customary to use a trace and hook line of fine
twisted wire and below the hook-link it is usual to have a
monofilament trace to the lead so that in the event of a 'hook-
up' or snagging of the weight, only the lead is lost.

Another method of using the paternoster is to cast in
leger fashion with the lead away from the angler and the line
tight. This probably means that although the bottom hook

58

may be on the bed, the higher hooks should be clear. In fresh-water angling this is termed 'low paternostering'. The sea angler often uses wire booms, or plastic booms with his pater-noster, and usually presents the tackle with two or three different kinds of bait, which he changes about in hook posi-tion so that he can more easily discover the type of bait the fish are taking and the depth at which the fish are feeding.

Sea anglers also have a version of the paternoster which is called a 'paternoster trot'. This consists of a trace to which several hooks are attached by means of a swivel. The lead is suspended on the running line about 6 inches below the swivel. The *illustration* shows how this tackle is made up, but though it can be successful, I feel that the angler who uses more than one hook at a time is being a bit of a dim-wit. First

Figure 18 A typical sea rig for pier and boat fishing. Termed a spreader (A) is the line; (B) the link swivel; (C) the central lead weight; (D) booms or arms of brass or stainless steel wire; (E) traces with baited hooks.

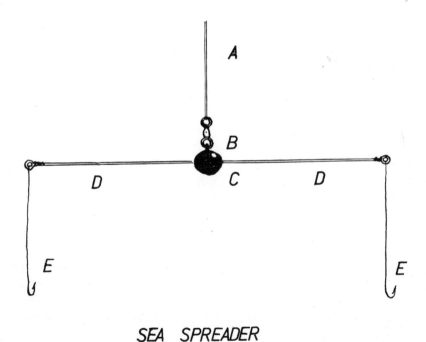

A

B

D   C   D

E   E

SEA SPREADER

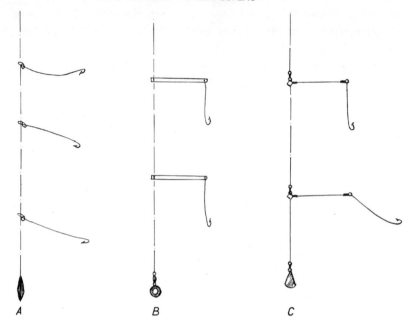

Figure 19 Sea angling paternosters. (A) uses nylon traces tied to running line; (B) uses plastic booms, and (C) uses stainless steel or brass boom arms mounted on swivels: this latter is known as a straight-pull paternoster.

of all he uses up more bait, secondly he takes longer to bait up (and this means less time when the hook is actually in the water), and thirdly, the more hooks on a line the greater the chances are of being caught up or snagged in underwater obstacles.

So far as the sea angler is concerned, the great advantage which the paternoster has over the leger is the fact that it keeps the bait off the bottom and away from marauding crabs.

Another form of paternostering, used by boat anglers at sea, though I have never come across it amongst freshwater boat anglers, is the 'spreader'. This consists of a boom with hooks hung from each end. The lead is attached to the centre of the boom and attached to the line by means of a swivel. The usual way to employ this method is to lower it into the water and then gently raise and lower it until it is found at what

60

depth the fish are interested; thereafter one angles at that depth. I think it could have possibilities in exploring deep holes in freshwater lakes and rivers.

'Wander' tackle

This is a method peculiar to sea angling and in pursuit of flat fish. This is, in reality, a form of roving sea leger. It consists of a hook, about size 4, baited with lugworm, a bunch of small white ragworms, or soft crab, and a nylon trace about 4 feet in length attached to the running line by means of a swivel. About 18 inches below the swivel a spiral or anti-kink lead is fixed weighing about 1 ounce. This tackle is used by casting and allowing it to sink to the bottom and then gradually recovering the line. The main lead stirs up the mud or sand on the bottom and this attracts flounders which then stalk the bait. The recovery rate is very slow and crabs can often be a nuisance. These may be defeated, however, if a small cork is attached to the trace about 8 inches above the hook, and this raises the baited hook from the bottom. When using this from the shore it is cast out and methodically recovered. When using it from a boat all that is necessary for the angler to do is to lower the hook over the side until the lead reaches the bottom and then allow it to drift along with the boat. If you are fishing from the bank of a creek or from a pier it is much better than either leger or paternoster as it allows you to cover the ground whereas the other rigs stay in one position.

10   Angling Techniques – Moving Baits

So far, apart from the wander tackle method mentioned in the last chapter, we have only considered angling methods where the bait is stationary, either suspended at a predetermined depth in the water, or on the bottom. Moving baits are used for those fish which are predators, that is, hunters, and the methods adopted include spinning, fly fishing, and 'sink and draw'.

Let's deal with this last method first.

This can be done to recover a static bait, i.e. by float fishing or by legering, or it can be used as a method in its own right. The method is simplicity itself. The bait is cast in, allowed to sink, and then the reel wound in a few turns: stop reeling in and allow the bait to sink again: wait a few seconds then start the procedure all over again. It is a useful method, and if a big lobworm or minnow is used for freshwater fishing, or a small fish, such as a sprat, used in sea fishing, the action imitates that of a sick or wounded fish. Barbel, chub, perch and pike will readily take by this method, and most sea fishes will investigate such a lure with fatal consequences for themselves.

Spinning

This method goes under different names according to the type of fishing one is doing. Spinning, in fresh water terms, means casting from the reel and recovering the bait. In sea angling this is called 'whiffing'. Sometimes freshwater anglers trail a moving lure behind a boat and this, not strictly angling in the true sense, is termed 'trolling': the same type of tactics employed by the sea angler would be termed 'railing'. I think that the only occasions when 'trolling' or 'railing' may be justifiably employed are (a) when trying to find an area in which fish are feeding, and then, having taken a fish by this method to continue angling by conventional means, and (b) when sea angling, and sailing to fishing grounds in a boat, to catch fish for bait on the way out to the spot.

Spinning is an exciting method of catching fish. Not everyone likes to sit and wait on a river or lake bank or on a pier, to wait for fish to take a static lure: for the angler who is much more active in temperament, especially on a cold day, spinning can be real fun. You seek out your fishes, you try to lure them by drawing a natural or artificial bait before them, inducing them to take the lure, and then fight the fish to the landing net.

Compared with bottom fishing equipment, spinning outfits are much more expensive. Not that the rods are really any dearer, but the extra outlay comes in the buying of lures. These can cost anything from 1s. 6d. to 15s. or more. Beautifully made, they are as much 'angler bait' as the beautiful and attractive floats which tempt anglers into buying them, even if they never use them! The real expense comes, of course, when expensive lures get lost, and if two or more should get lost on one fishing outing, then it does become an expensive day.

A spinning rod may be much shorter than a bottom rod. It will probably be from 4 feet to 6 feet in length and must be stiff enough to cast a bait of over an ounce in weight, but whippy enough to have action right through to the butt. Angling conditions, again, dictate the type of spinning rod to be used. A reservoir or a river with a high bank will need a longer rod than a low bank: otherwise retrieving the lure after each cast does become difficult.

Though the closed-face reel is popular with some enthusiasts, and I am one, the multiplier really comes into its own for spinning work. Here the rate of recovery makes the angling task easier. Recovery of a spinning lure by means of a centre-pin reel is a long, tiring business – especially at the end of a long, long day. The more so, if no fish have been taken!

One of the attractions of spinning is that it is a clean business. There are no messy morsels of cut-up bait to worry about, boxes of maggots, or bags of worms. On top of this, spinning tackle takes up a lot less room. There is no need for bags of groundbait: there is no need for stool or portable seat and a whole selection of lures will easily fit into a small box carried in the angler's pocket.

Lures can be spun at all depths. From the surface, with floating lures such as 'plugs', to way deep down on or near the bottom. Other types of lure may be spun in mid-water and a full description of artificial lures used in spinning, and flights on to which dead natural baits may be used, is given in the chapter on Artificial Baits.

Spinning is NOT a matter of chuck it and chance it. The water temperature, speed of current or tide, and the time of the year all have a bearing on spinning conditions. For example, in cold weather the fish lie deeper in the water and a heavier lure is necessary. When fishing across a current it is usual to make the first cast across the current and then gradually vary the angle of casts until one is finally casting downstream and almost parallel with the bank.

When spinning there is rarely need for the angler to actually strike. The movement of the lure through the water usually does the trick, and all that is necessary to get the hook firmly home into the jaw of a taking fish is to lightly increase the pressure on the rod.

There are two or three methods one can employ to recover the lure. Firstly, there is the straightforward winding in of the reel after the lure has reached the correct depth. This means that the bait is recovered at a constant speed. Secondly, the lure may be recovered a little at a time on the 'sink and draw' principle, but the speed can be varied between the recovery periods and the lure speeded up and slowed down as well as allowed to rise and fall. Thirdly, the lure may be recovered at varying speeds and the rod tip moved up and down so that not only does the lure appear to dart, but also wobbles about.

IT IS ABSOLUTELY NECESSARY TO KEEP WINDING IN THE BAIT UNTIL THE VERY LAST MOMENT. I cannot emphasise this too strongly because a bait is often taken just when the angler is ready to lift it from the water. This is especially so when casting over shallow water into deep water, for a frightened or immature fish will naturally make for the shallows when pursued by a predator, and it will be in the shallows when the bite is finally made.

It is a good idea to change the lures over every so often from right hand spin to one with a left hand spin. This takes out any twist which might have been put into the line in spite of anti-kink devices and swivels used in the tackle make-up.

Spinning from the beach is a good form of sea fishing and this is known as 'surf casting'. A good glass fibre rod about 7 feet in length is ideal. The rod must be sturdy, very flexible, and I recommend the short length because one is not distance casting at all, and will rarely cast beyond 40 yards. Using the appropriate lure the angler will be searching within the shallows and casting behind the breakers where the larger species of bass are wont to hunt.

For surf spinning the reel should be placed fairly high on the butt of the rod and the rod held with the right hand immediately under the reel. The butt of the rod should be held by the left hand, almost at the end.

The rod tip is brought back until the lure almost touches the ground and then, with the right hand acting as a pivot, the left hand pushes the butt away from you. Now cast by pulling back the butt with the left hand, at the same time pushing the upper part of the rod away with the right hand. Follow through until the line runs out straight from the rod tip. When the bait hits the water raise the rod to about 45° and start re-winding. Vary the rewinding recovery rate during the retrieve and work the bait at differing depths.

Spinning can be done from a centre-pin reel much in the sink and draw manner, and using the forefinger brake on the drum.

Whatever the style or tackle used there is one golden rule: in fast-moving waters the lure must be recovered at a slower rate than in slow or still waters, otherwise it will rise to the surface and remain there. Again, when using artificial lures, on a dark day use a bright lure, on a bright day, a duller coloured bait will be appropriate.

Before going out to the waterside or seaside and practising spinning, it is best to get a little practice in on dry land. One can practise casting at a given target; practise casting with either hand, and sideways, and even underarm, until one is able to cope with all sorts of angling conditions.

Remember also it is important to learn to cast with the wind, against the wind, and at all angles across it.

11 Natural Baits – Freshwater Angling

There are so many different kinds of baits which the angler can use for fishing that it seems incredible that anglers can actually find themselves without any bait! Yet this does happen – so beware the scrounger who comes up to you at the waterside and tries to borrow some of your bait. He is either downright miserly, thoroughly lazy, or a mere sponger.

Most anglers seem to have their own special preference for a bait and many are the cunning mixtures they work into them: almost like the alchemist of the Middle Ages. The most popular freshwater angling baits are bread paste, bread cubes, maggots (or gentles), worms, grubs, small live fish, small dead fish, stewed wheat, barley, hemp, elderberries, and various insects. Even the silkweed found on weirs, and pieces of macaroni and cheese are used successfully.

Maggots or gentles

These are very popular and there is a whole industry devoted to their raising. Maggot factories, they could almost be called maggot ranches, provide tackle shops with millions of these creatures annually, and they may be supplied plain, coloured, or natural! They are often dyed different colours, pink, yellow, green, and red being the most popular. They may be advertised as 'liver bred' or 'ordinary' but, regardless of all this they can form a very expensive item in the angler's requirements for a day's fishing. At 6s. to 10s. per tin, it is not uncommon for a keen angler, especially a match fisherman, to use up to £2 or more worth of maggots in a weekend – and that's a lot of maggots.

The young angler usually buys 6d. to 1s. worth of maggots and does very well out of them. The real expense in maggot

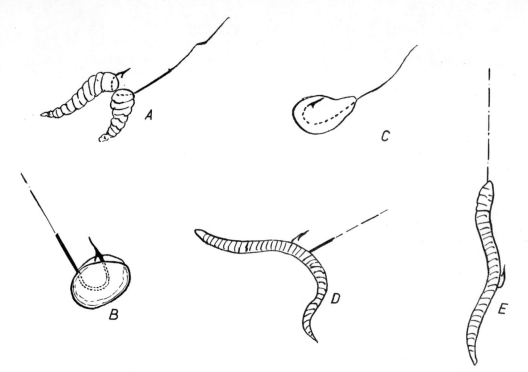

Figure 20 Showing how some baits should be placed on the hook.
(A) a hook baited with two gentles or maggots; (B) How a single
hempseed is placed on the hook; (C) Correct moulding of bread paste
round hook, and (D) and (E) methods of mounting lobworms.

buying lies in the huge quantities which are used as ground
bait: it is not the maggots on the hooks which are expensive,
but the maggots thrown into the water.

Contrary to what many people, especially the ladies,
believe the maggots are about the cleanest of all live baits.
They are generally classified into three groups known as
'squats', which are the larvae of the common housefly:
'pinkies' which come from the greenbottle: and 'livers' which
come from the bluebottle. When, an angler goes in for match
or competition work he generally uses the larger maggots,
livers, specials and pinkies, as hook bait and uses the 'squats'
for ground-baiting.

But whatever maggot is used, it must be lively when it is
presented to the fish and care must be exercised in putting it

68

on the hook. To bait the hook with maggots or gentles put the hook point through the fat end of the maggot: if two or more are being used, and quite often a bunch of maggots on a hook is a really good bait, the top maggot may be put on lengthwise and the others transversely, but, and this is very important, the point of the hook must show through the skin of the last maggot.

Chrysalids

Maggots which are left in the bait box generally turn into chrysalids. This is the next stage before the grub becomes a fly. These make a very effective bait for roach, dace, and rudd and sometimes, if the normal maggot has failed to take fish, two or three chrysalids on a hook will change the luck of the angler. However, they are more difficult to place on a hook because they are not so tough as the original grub and break open very easily.

If the chrysalid sinks, it becomes known as a 'caster' and it pays the angler to go through his box of chrysalids sorting them out into sinkers and floaters. Some anglers discard the floating chrysalids or add a dust shot to them to make them sink.

Grubs

These are a natural follow-on bait from the maggot or gentle. There are many different kinds of grubs to be found, and the two most highly sought after are the dock or docken grub, which is found under dock plants, and the wasp grub. It's a highly risky business, however, collecting wasp grubs because smoking out a wasp's nest is apt to be more than lively, and not to be recommended. If one can buy wasp grubs, though, they should be baked slightly to toughen them up before placing them on the hook. Caterpillars also come into the grub category and if the angler drops them lightly on to the water with an unweighted line, then they become a popular bait for chub.

Worms

In the public mind, the worm is the typical and most popular fishing bait. Earthworms are suitable for most fishes from roach to pike and salmon.

The most popular worms are brandling, red, and lob and they are fairly easy to obtain from tackle shops. The brandling can be found in manure and compost heaps, but before using should be placed in damp moss for a couple of days to 'scour' them. The largest worm is the lobworm, and this is generally found on lawns after dark. I always manage to get a good supply of these from my allotment, and they, in common with the red worm, may be trapped by placing sacking or old carpeting on the ground, under which they will congregate, if it is kept damp. Lobs may also be found on a damp night by the aid of a flash lamp.

There are two methods of hooking the worms. It may be caught underneath the skin, or threaded on and worked up the hook until only a fraction of an inch remains free. But, whatever worm is used, it must be lively: dead and damaged worms are useless on the hook and should be discarded.

Meal worms

Few creatures repel me, but I always think that these are simply vile looking creatures! They are to be bought from pet shops, rather than tacklists, as they are used to feed curious pets which some people acquire from time to time. They do, I am assured, make a good bait for roach and dace, but they are quite dear to buy.

Live and dead fish

Fish are cannibals – they will feed not only on other species but also upon their own. Presented dead or alive, minnows, bleak, small roach and dace, are excellent baits for pike and perch. Dead natural fish may be used as spinning baits and legered sprats and kippers make good bait for pike.

A lively minnow, hooked through the lip, and dropped by

paternoster into a deep hole is a very effective bait for perch: sometimes the fun becomes fast and furious and the bait is barely down to the right depth before it is seized.

When pike fishing with live bait, it is the considered opinion of the expert pike angler that the dace is the most active and useful. The pike takes its prey sideways in its jaws and swallows it after it has turned it head downwards and started to run. This is the moment when the angler should strike to drive the hook home into the pike's hard bony mouth. When fishing with a live bait the float moves about on the surface, but this is only the movement of the hooked bait: this movement must therefore be disregarded until it is seen to bob under two or three times. This is a signal that a pike has attacked the bait; suddenly the float will go under the surface and start to glide off. Whatever you do DO NOT STRIKE at this moment, hold your breath and, like the free-fall parachutist, count up to ten slowly, and then strike. From that moment on the battle should have commenced between yourself and the pike and you'll find out what it is like to meet a powerful fish. But don't forget, let the rod take the strain and in time the pike will tire and be able to be brought in.

A dead bait is a terrific attraction for pike and for eels, too. A herring is a good bait for a pike and success is fairly well assured if a herring or sprat is cut up into small pieces and ground baited near the dead bait.

Cereal baits

Stewed wheat and barley are good baits and are clean and easy to use. Whenever a fish takes a hook baited with wheat or barley, it is generally a fairly hooked fish. The grain is prepared by soaking for a day and then stewing it until the grains burst open. Sometimes it can be prepared in a vacuum flask. When using these baits bait the hook with a single large grain and make sure that the point of the hook is showing through the soft skin of the grain.

Hemp seed is another popular bait. But don't get confused with Indian hemp, or dope, hemp seed is sold in pet shops for feeding pets, and also in angling tackle shops for fishing purposes. It is prepared in a similar way to wheat, and is a very killing bait – so good in fact that on many waters it has been banned.

Elderberries

These are easily collected during the summer on bushes in their wild state, but can also be bought by the lazy fisherman, ready preserved in jars. When they are ripe and black they are a really good bait for roach and dace and they should be placed on the hook, size 14, by piercing the skin with the barb showing. It is probably best to put two or more berries on one hook and now and again throw in a handful as ground bait. Elderberries are not fished on the bottom, but just below the surface.

Bread and cheese

These two everyday commodities are excellent baits. Indeed, a whole book could be written about their uses and preparation. Bread paste is made from fairly new loaves. The crusts are removed after which the bread is placed in a cloth and then in water. The cloth and bread are next removed and the surplus water squeezed out by twisting the cloth, after which the wet bread is kneaded into a paste. The essential thing to bear in mind is that the hands must be absolutely clean when kneading the bread; diesel oil fumes from your model aircraft or motorboat must be removed, otherwise the fish will be repelled by and not attracted to the paste bait.

To put the paste on to the hook, roll it between the finger and thumb until it looks like a pea. The hook is then buried deeply within this dough pea so that the whole of the bend and the point are covered. This is vital. Anglers who use paste and leave a lot of hook showing will never catch fish: nor will anglers who use a simply enormous blob of paste and bury a small hook within it.

Anglers have different recipes which they add to the paste. Some add a little cotton wool to make it stay better on the hook: some add scented concoctions: but, all in all, if pre-

72

sented properly, the bread paste itself will do the job quite well.

Bread may also be used in cubes. This is made from crusts. The crust should be cut about $\frac{1}{4}$ inch thick, placed on a damp cloth, covered with another damp cloth, and pressed overnight between a couple of boards. The resultant 'sheet' of bread can then be cut into cubes.

Bread crumbs, whether from stale bread, or by deliberately drying a loaf and pulverising it, make an excellent 'cloud' bait. This, thrown into the water, remains in suspension for quite a while and attracts fish to the area. The main bait is then thrown into this cloud and the angler can hopefully begin his fishing.

Cheese may be worked into a paste and used by itself or in conjunction with bread. Chub have a partiality for it, and I have also known river trout take it.

Finally, silkweed. This is a natural bait, found on weirs. There is no specific way of obtaining it and then baiting up the hook with it; but the job is done very simply by just casting the hook into the silkweed. A few strands are generally left hanging on the hook which is then fished downstream with float tackle. This is a worthwhile method to use because fish will only feed on silkweed if it is in the area. It is easy to obtain, and doesn't cost one decimal coin!

Other baits

Fish like to take all sorts of baits: grasshoppers and caddis grubs: bacon rind: pieces of sausage, and even whole sausages: and even macaroni can be used. Wherever there are fishing waters, there are generally some natural baits available within the area: whether one nets or traps minnows or tadpoles, catches small insects, uses silkweed or berries, no angler need ever complain that he is without bait.

12   Natural Baits – Sea Fishing

Just as in the last chapter I referred to the great number of natural baits which can be used by the freshwater fisherman, equally so there is never any excuse for the sea angler to be without any bait.

Most natural saltwater baits fall into two groups: worms and fishes. In fishes are included shellfishes and crustaceans.

Chief of course on the list of natural baits are fish baits. These should be as fresh as possible, and oily fishes make the best baits. In order of preference they should read, herring, garfish, pilchards, mackerel, sprats, and eels. For very large fish, such as tope and conger and sharks, whole fish may be used, but for average sea angling it is usual to make one fish (unless it is a sprat) into several pieces of bait.

When preparing fish baits the angler must have a good sharp knife, a bait board on which to cut up the bait because it is not possible to do this on a sandy or pebbly beach, and it certainly should not be done on a pier walkway or seat, and a box in which to put the cut up fish pieces.

The procedure is quite straightforward and must be methodical. First of all remove the scales from the fish by scraping, then lay it flat on the bait board and, commencing at the tail, cut along the backbone to the head. Insert the knife beneath the backbone and lift it out from the flesh.

Now, place one half of the fish skin side downwards on to the board and cut into diagonal pieces, as shown in the drawing, each about one inch in width. The average-sized mackerel will give you 8 or 9 such strips from each side. There is another type of fish bait known as a 'last' or 'lask'. This is made by removing two or three inches of triangular shaped skin from the tail (see drawing) which should have all the flesh scraped from it.

74

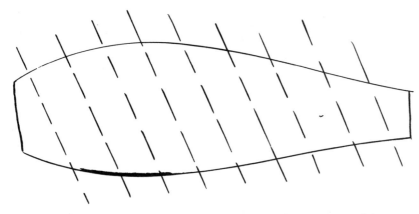

Figure 21 Showing how strips should be cut from fish to make fish bait strips for mounting on to hook.

Here a word of advice – don't throw the entrails and bits of useless fish away – you are going to need them for ground bait. Very small fish may be used whole, and sprat-sized fish may be slit down the middle and half a fish used at a time.

To bait a fish slice on to the hook – push the point of the hook through the fleshy side of the darker portion of the skin, bringing it through to the other side, and then hook it through the lighter colour (see drawing). The 'lask' is mounted by

Figure 22 Showing area (shaded) to be cut from tail portion of fish to make a skin lask or last.

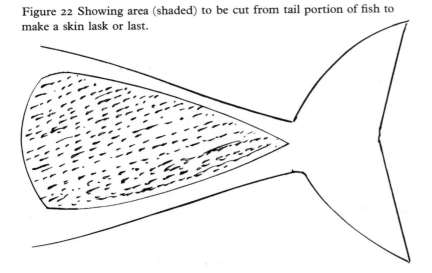

75

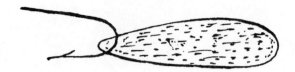

Figure 23 (Upper) How a lask is mounted on the hook, and (lower) correct way of inserting hook into fish strip bait.

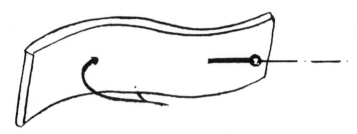

merely putting it over the point of the hook with the base of the triangle flowing behind it. A large fish, or a fish with a large mouth, such as cod or bass, require large hooks, and want large portions of bait. Sand-eels make excellent baits and may be used alive or dead. When used as a live bait the hook point should be inserted into the mouth of the fish and out through the gills. For dead bait mounting the sand-eel should be mounted on to a single hook inserted through the mouth and emerging one third way back from the head.

Octopi and squid are first class baits, except for one thing – they go high very quickly, and how they go high! The squid and the cuttle fish, expecially the latter, may be seen quite often floating in thousands upon the sea. The flesh itself is a good bait, and the tentacles also, are first class. The conger eel is very partial to a piece of fresh squid or cuttle, and bass, pollack, and coalfish will take it when presented as a spinning lure.

Shellfish

There are different opinions about these. Some anglers think they are good – others have found them useless and haven't hesitated to say so. But, though they cannot be regarded as certain killers, they are good standby baits. They are clean and

76

easy to collect and keep, but they are not easy to place on a hook. The limpet can be an absolutely first class bait, sometimes – on other occasions it can be as useless as a bait can be.

Limpets do present a bit of a problem with their collection because they don't get their name for nothing. Once they are touched they simply get down to the business of staying put, and nothing will move them. However, a sudden tap from the side with a small pebble, hammer, or sheath knife will generally move them so that they can easily be picked off. In point of fact, I have often gathered limpets by just giving them a sudden sideways push with the forefinger.

To use limpets as bait – first take it from the shell. The creature inside will consist of two portions, one hard and one soft. Bring the hook point through the soft portion and press it into the hard bit. It is not necessary to follow the practice which some anglers adopt of tying the bait on with a piece of wool.

Mussels are probably the best of the shell fish baits and are very easily collected from piers, sea walls, and from banks of mussels known as 'scaurs'. Cod have a preference for mussels collected from estuaries and if the angler is fishing in an area much frequented by dogfishes, then he should use mussels as these fish don't like them. Opening mussels brings its own problems. First of all examine a mussel. It will be seen to be straight on one side and curved on the other. Hold the mussel with the narrow pointed edge in the palm of the hand and gently push the upper shell sideways. Now, put the point of a knife into this tiny opening and pass the blade between the body of the mussel and the lower portion of the shell. This enables you to cut the fish's attachment from the shell. This is done by cutting along one side of the powerful muscle which holds the two shell halves together. The mussel itself must remain unbroken in the shell half.

Placing the mussel on the hook is a second problem. Press the hook through the mussel from side to side and press the point into the white muscle which had to be cut in order to open the shell. If this is done properly the bait will stay on the hook without having to be tied on with any thread or wool.

Another good shell fish to use is the whelk. But this fish has a terribly tough shell and it needs a good strong blow from a hammer to get the whelk out. Pinwinkles, or winkles, will do if necessary, but are not a terribly successful bait. Probably the best shell fish of all is the solen or razor fish. These are dug for with a narrow spade and get their name from their resemblance to the old-fashioned cut-throat razor.

Sea worms

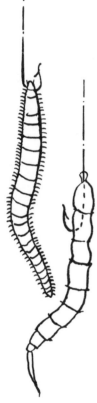

Always popular baits. King ragworms and lugworms will be found advertised in angling papers; they can be ordered through the post and delivered per passenger train with carriage charges extra. Sea worm digging is an industry by itself and hundreds of thousands of worms are sold weekly. In some districts the local authorities prevent the indiscriminate digging of sea worms and issue permits to professionals only.

Sea worms are expensive baits to buy and in many cases the cost of a day's sea worms for bait will be greater than the cost of hooks and terminal tackle. Assuming that an angler orders, and receives, his bait in good time, he must allow for a certain percentage of casualties amongst them before he can use them, and this in itself increases the cost of the bait. But the beginner will find, if he tries to start digging his own bait, that the charges are not so dear as he imagined, for he will get more aches to his back than worms in the box on his first few expeditions. Lugworms live in the sand. They eat their way through it and after taking their food from it, pass it through their bodies where it is thrown up on to the surface of the beach in the form of a coil of sand. This is known as a cast.

About a foot to a foot and a half from the cast there will be found a blow-hole and the lugworm lies midway between these two points in a U-shaped tunnel. The angler after lug has to dig methodically, but once he has started digging he must do so quickly because the lug can burrow like lightning. Using either a very narrow-bladed spade or a three-tined fork, the angler should stand astride the cast and blow-hole. Then he should insert the tool into the sand about 6 inches in front of the blow-hole and remove a spit of sand. The worm should now be in the U-channel *behind* the fork or spade. The angler

Figure 24 Hooks baited with sea worms. (Left) Using ragworm, and (right) with lugworm.

78

should now dig a channel the width of the tool in steps towards the cast and as soon as the track of the worm is found the spade or fork should be inserted quickly behind the worm which is then lifted clear of the hole. But one must be careful not to damage the worm because not only does it become useless for bait but it exudes a nasty reddish-yellow fluid which stains the fingers.

Lug can be kept alive for a few days in a wooden box of wet sand or seaweed, stored in a cool place. Dead and sickly worms should be removed immediately.

Ragworms, on the other hand, though they lie deep in the mud, do not make a cast but they do make a blow-hole. They do not burrow as deeply as the lugworm and may be dug for in a similar way. The ragworm looks rather like a centipede, or a cross between a worm and a centipede for it has a pair of feet attached to each body segment. It is a beautifully coloured creature but, a word of caution, the head holds a pair of pincers which can deliver a sharp, blood-drawing nip to the careless handler.

Some species of rag may be found under stones and in the cracks of rocks, whilst one species usually takes up residence behind a hermit crab living in a discarded whelk shell. Small white rag are to be found in the ooze of harbours and creeks and these are a very popular bait with the mullet hunter.

Crabs, shrimps and prawns

Nothing makes the sea angler see red quicker than the marauding crabs which steal his bait. But, on the other hand, when crab is used as a bait by the angler it is a very good one.

The ordinary green crab is to be found in almost every tidal pool, or under the larger stones on a pebbly beach. It is a very good bait, and providing it is not much larger than a shilling across can be baited whole on the hook. The green crab is an obliging chap for when he grows larger he grows out of his shell, which he casts and then goes to hide in a nook or cranny until the new shell forms to grow hard body armour again. During this period it is known as soft-back crab and this is a most attractive bait. If it is of any size at all it must be

79

cut up into pieces for placing on the hook. Large crabs, even green crabs with hard backs, can be killed, mashed and placed with fish entrails etc., into a ground bait mixture.

The hermit crab is a good bait but not always easy to obtain. The tail is particularly attractive to whiting and flat fish.

Shrimps and prawns may be used either as live or dead bait. Most sea fish such as mullet, bass, flatties, and eels, will take them. If they are used alive they should be hooked through the tail: if used as a dead bait they should first be boiled and then mounted head foremost.

Just as the freshwater angler uses ground bait, so the sea fisherman can, in fact should, do the same. Portions of fish can be cut up and placed on rocks where the tide and waves will wash them into the fishing area: portions can be thrown or lowered by a bag to the baited hook, or a rubby-dubby bag can be placed in the sea near the baited hook.

There are lots more baits which can be used by the enterprising angler. Pieces of bacon and bacon skin can be cut into a squid-like shape and trailed through the water: mullet will prove partial to macaroni paste, and flounders in estuarial waters will take earthworms.

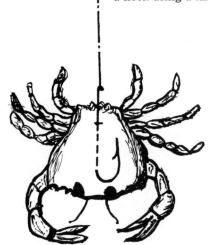

Figure 25 The correct way to bait a hook using a small crab.

13   Artificial Baits

The artificial baits or lures described in this chapter will be found suitable, sometimes with slight modifications, for both freshwater and saltwater fishing. Artificial lures are generally classified into spinning, wobbling, spoon, plug baits, and flies.

First of all, I strongly suggest that the angler should purchase only those artificial baits which have an absolute minimum of hooks. I have seen some lures simply festooned with hooks – and this greatly increases their prospects of being caught up in weeds or other obstacles, foul-hooking a fish, or impaling the hand of the angler himself, to say nothing of the tangle they can make in a tackle box if through some mischance it should be dropped. In practice a lure with one single hook is, without any doubt whatever, the best proposition.

Figure 26 Two artifical lures: these are spoon baits. (A) is a Kidney spoon, and (B) a Colorado spoon with spinning vanes at the head.

A

B

Today many lures are sold which make use of treble hooks. During the past few years many angling practices have gone out of use or favour because they were either cruel, as in gorge-baiting for pike, or inefficient. Today, with modern equipment, modern materials for rods, easily manipulated reels, superb lines, there is no room at all for the treble hook, or even the double hook. Such hooks are out of date, complete anachronisms and, furthermore if a taking fish should close his mouth upon a treble and the line break, then it is doomed to die from starvation or fall prey to some other predatory fish as its condition weakens.

As fish take the lures from behind, that is, by chasing and overtaking their prey, a single hook is perfectly adequate for all spinning and other artificial baits.

Let us break down artificial lures into separate categories and deal with them in turn: these are

(1) Spoons and wobblers
(2) Artificial fish
(3) Plug baits
(4) Feathered lures

Spoons and wobblers

These baits when drawn through the water wobble and twist about in an erratic path and, as the term spoon indicates, they are generally manufactured in the shape of that article. In fact, quite good artificial lures can be made from discarded kitchen spoons.

Spoons and wobblers, the latter being flattish metal or plastic plates, diamond, oblong, or oval shaped, and bent or twisted so that they twirl about in the water when being recovered, vary in size from about $\frac{3}{4}$ inch to several inches in length. They all vary slightly in shape, and the 'Kidney' spoon, for example, has the appearance of that organ. The so-called 'Colorado' spoon has two vanes at its head, a leaded bar through the long axis, and a hook at the rear on to which a tuft of red wool is attached. The 'Colorado' is generally painted red inside, but the outside is left shiny.

The sea angler uses a special technique with a spoon bait when fishing for flounders. This is known as 'baited spoon spinning'. The outfit consists of a spoon body attached by a spring link and swivel to the trace. The spoon, which is generally white in colour, is attached only by the head, and a single large hook which is attached to a series of swivels linked together for the whole length of the spoon body, stands well clear of the spoon itself. This hook is baited with lug-worm, ragworm, or other bait, and is a very successful method of catching the flounder.

Artificial fish

These are shaped to resemble small fish and vary from the so-called 'Devon' minnow, made of metal to the rubber or plastic 'sand-eel' used by the sea fisher. The 'Devon' is usually a small torpedo-shaped lure, from 2 to 4 inches in length. It may be gold, silver, or blue in colour. At the head are a pair of vanes which cause it to revolve around a central wire mount when it is pulled through the water. As in the 'Colorado' spoon and 'baited spoon' the hook is mounted well

Figure 27 Two metal artificial lures. (A) is the Devon minnow, and (B) a flat wobbler. These may be used for coarse and game fishing, and also for sea angling.

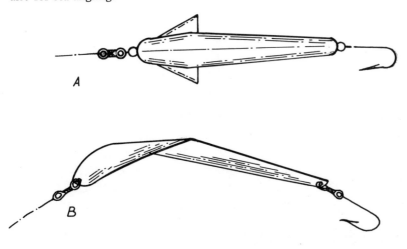

A

B

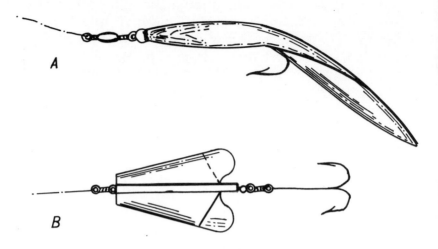

Figure 28 Two sea angling artificial lures. (A) A rubber or plastic imitation sand-eel. (B) A mackerel spinner.

to the rear of the minnow body. The rubber or plastic sand-eel varies from a simple rubber or plastic tube mounted on to a bent wire with a swivel at the head and a hook hidden within the body but with the barb and point protruding. Sometimes the lure will have a small pair of vanes attached to the head. It may be white, black, red, or green in colour. On the other hand, the sand-eel may be a very fine imitation of the real thing, made from a plastic body, and costing quite a bit more to purchase. The artificial sand-eel is a very good spinning bait for bass.

Under the heading of artificial fish may be included the mackerel spinner – this is an arrow-shaped piece of metal with the rear portion bent into vanes. It is mounted on to a flight containing one hook. Sometimes silver or gold, some-times dual coloured, e.g. red and white or blue and white, they are about the cheapest of all spinning lures to buy – and very successful too. An alternative is the 'Dazzler' – this also imitates the action of a small fish and merely consists of three or more pairs of brightly coloured vanes mounted in front of a hook, and attached to the trace by means of a swivel. This is also a good mackerel lure.

In addition to these somewhat crude imitations of fish, there are on the market today wonderful models of fish, made from plastic, and coloured most realistically: they certainly look well in the tackle box, but they are quite costly to lose.

Chief amongst these artificial fishes are the plastic soft-back crabs which one sees on sale in tackle shops – I feel certain that people must purchase them, otherwise the manufacturer would not go to the trouble of making them and marketing them – but I have never purchased one nor tested one out so I cannot comment on their efficiency. Plastic worms, plastic maggots, and imitation beetles and frogs are also available. I have tried out the imitation beetles and frogs and found them very effective when trout fishing, and I do not doubt but that in conditions when the water is 'thick' artificial worms and maggots, especially if scented, might well do the trick.

Plug baits

These are very successful lures indeed. They can be used against all predatory fish, both in fresh water and in the sea, and come in a variety of patterns and sizes to suit almost every angling condition.

A plug bait may consist of a wooden or transparent plastic body and is usually built to represent a small fish or other aquatic creature. A sloping nose, or vane, is the mechanism which causes the lure to dive below the surface when it is drawn through the water, behaving like the vanes on a submarine. Most plug baits are of the floating type, that is, they are exactly the opposite of the metal spinner which sinks when cast into the water but can be made to rise when recovered. The plug usually floats on the surface when it is cast and only begins to dive when it is being recovered. The plug may have a single, simple body or be joined in two or three, or even have many joints to represent an eel. The action of all plugs is to represent a frightened, wounded, or sickly fish.

Some plugs are used only on the surface and they may be used successfully amongst feeding shoals of mackerel.

From a simple plug with a shaped head causing it to wobble and dive, the plug may be built from plastic and even

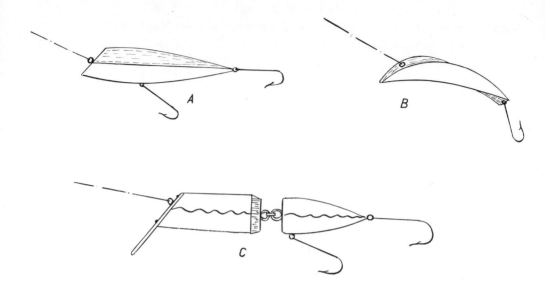

Figure 29 Examples of plug lures. (A) This is a simple single bodied diving lure; (B) This plug is used on the surface; (C) A jointed wobbling diving plug with diving vane at the head.

have adjustable vanes which enable it to be retrieved at a pre-determined depth. The great advantage that the plug bait has over the metal one is its inborn property of rising to the surface whenever the angler stops reeling in. This enables an angler to spin for fish over the tops of weeds without the same fear of losing the lure which he would experience if using a conventional spoon or Devon.

Feathered lures

These are of two types. Flies for fishing for game fish and coarse fish in fresh water, are dressed (usually) to represent natural insects and may be presented wet, that is sunken beneath the surface, or dry, floating on the surface. This is a specialist form of angling and I will deal with it briefly in a separate chapter. The other type of feathered lure consists of plastic or natural feathers tied to large sea hooks, either singly, or on a long line with a half-dozen or more hooks. This is usually trailed behind a boat, or cast from the beach and drawn

86

across the water. It is a very successful method of catching mackerel and other surface feeding fish but is rather a crude way of fishing, and it is difficult to class it as 'sporting'. One lure — yes: but a whole string jigged up and down — no!

14 · Fishing from Boats

This chapter applies to all forms of boat fishing, both on inland waters, and sea angling. There are obvious advantages of using a boat for fishing: it enables one to get to points where fish congregate and which are otherwise inaccessible to the shore angler. But I think that too many anglers go far too lightheartedly into the business of fishing from boats.

First of all – no one should go fishing from a boat without first of all learning to swim. I don't think that I can stress this point too thoroughly. For that matter even the bank fisherman should also know enough about swimming to get himself out of trouble if he should accidentally fall in. Being able to swim may not only save your own life, but you may perhaps save someone else's: and it will certainly prevent someone perhaps losing his or her own life in trying to rescue you because you can't swim. No, the angler who is physically unable to swim, or too lazy, or too scared to learn, should keep away from the water, as otherwise he is being not only stupid, but selfish as well. Secondly, when going afloat, especially on large lakes and lochs, and certainly on the sea, some form of life saving jacket should be worn at *all* times. It is remarkably easy to fall overboard and most boatmen take a ducking sometime or other. Never go out in a boat without having some practical experience of handling one, even a small rowing dinghy, because it is easy to get into trouble. Moving about wrongly can capsize a craft or throw one into the water, while the loss of an oar can be fatal.

Certainly one should never embark on off-shore boating on the coast without having lessons from a properly qualified person, and it is advisable, if one is not so experienced, to book a place on a boat which specially caters for anglers and angling parties. There are plenty of these advertised in the angling papers, and local clubs will soon put you in touch with the right person.

When going sea fishing with a boatman it is as well to understand the position regarding the fish caught: usually all fish caught become the property of the boatman, and he allows you to take some away with you. But get this settled first, it saves a lot of arguments later.

If you are going to sea in a boat you have hired, then make sure that it is in good condition, that there is a baler available in case water is shipped, that the anchor rope is not frayed, and that the oars, rowlocks and pins are sound. And, above all, beware of two very dangerous conditions – the offshore wind and the sudden fog. The offshore wind is dangerous because it may only be gentle and the angler gradually drifts farther and farther out to sea before he realises just how far out his position is: and conditions may be such that a combination of wind and currents or tides can prevent him rowing back. Fog, of course, is always dangerous, and in hazy conditions it is best not to venture out, except in company of more experienced, preferably professional, sailors.

Inland fishing by boat can be extremely pleasant. On a hot summer's day it is ideal to relax in an anchored boat, taking in the sun and not particularly caring about the fishing, until the day begins to die and the fish come on to the feed. Fishing at anchor for perch in deep holes is great fun, but even better is fishing by allowing the boat to drift, that is, by turning it sideways to the wind and allowing it to drift along. This enables you to search and cover a fairly large area of water, and then, having found a good spot where fish are on the feed, to gently lower the anchor and start angling in earnest.

If two or more anglers are in a boat and one has a bite, then the other anglers should reel in their lines to give him a chance to play and land his fish. If there are only two anglers in a boat, they should fish from either end and, above all, one must avoid moving about in the boat, talking, banging the sides and bottom, because sound and vibrations travel and these put the fish down.

One fine little problem arises when playing a fish from a boat and he goes under it! Do not attempt to pull the fish

back from under the boat by reeling, instead point the rod tip round either stem or stern (front or back) and gradually play the fish to the windward side. It is sometimes a little difficult when the boat is anchored and the fish takes a circular dive round the anchor rope – but, as I have said earlier, angling is fun.

When sea fishing, do not do so from too small a boat; only a year or so back an angler was drowned when a conger eel he had caught managed to tip him off balance and throw him into the sea from a very small dinghy: and remember, too, that some sea fish are quite large and can actually tow your craft! This happened to me once in Scottish waters when fishing for coalfish I accidentally foul-hooked a basking shark! It wasn't so much the towing I took a dislike to as the manner in which the bow began to go to the waterline when he started to go to the bottom – he was probably unaware of what was happening – but I had to cut the line otherwise the boat would have been swamped. I wasn't very brave at that moment, I can tell you.

Sea anglers usually find that the fish they take from boats are larger than fish taken from the shore and piers: specimen lists, and medals which are awarded, take this factor into consideration.

Plate 4 (*opposite*) The use of a boat enables one to fish in otherwise inaccessible places.

15   Big Game Fishing

Until recent years one only thought of big game fishing as the sport of the wealthy adventurer who sought Tiger Sharks in tropical waters, or fished for tunny, sailfish and swordfish in the Gulf of Florida. Our only big game fishing carried on in Britain was for the giant Tunny, in the North Sea. But now, with more and more boats getting to sea, and with more and more anglers exploring hitherto unconsidered British waters, we are finding big game fish right on our own coastline. Sharks, blue shark, thresher, porbeagle, even the ferocious mako are on our list: many southern resorts now include shark-fishing as their attractions and so far, touch wood, there is no instance of a British shark attacking and killing a bather. The dread cry 'Shark! Shark! of Australian beaches only brings hope and expectation into the heart of the modern British off-shore fisherman. Though, too, shark can be caught from the shore, and there is one specialist in Ireland who catches enormous bags of large sharks this way.

Sharks, though, are but one species of big game fish to be taken in British saltwater. What other species are there? Well, there is, for example, the Conger Eel. This fish is a great fighter, and can be pretty fearsome too. His weight could well go over the hundredweight! Then there is the Tope, a favourite small member of the shark family, the Skates and Rays, and some larger members of the dogfishes. As to weights of these fishes, some recorded weights have been:

Blue Shark – over 200 pounds
Mako Shark – over 400 pounds
Porbeagle Shark – over 300 pounds
Thresher Shark – almost 300 pounds
Conger Eel – over 80 pounds

Bull Huss (the Greater Spotted Dogfish) – over 20
    pounds
Common Skate – 200 pounds
Sting Ray – almost 60 pounds
Thornback Ray – nearly 40 pounds
Tunny (but hardly likely to be fished for under present-
    day conditions) – over 800 pounds
Blonde Ray – nearly 30 pounds

So you will see that though most specimens will be much
below these weights, there are, none the less some pretty big
fish awaiting capture.

Shark fishing

I will deal with this only briefly, because most anglers will
only have an opportunity to go shark-fishing perhaps once a
year, when on holiday. Most beginners are taken out by an
experienced boatman in a motorboat specially equipped for
the purpose. As may be expected, the tackle must be strong,
and the rod comparatively short. The reel and line must be
able to withstand tremendous strain and it is customary for
the angler to fish from a special angler's chair with a harness
which fits over him. A wire trace is necessary as a shark spins
and can break it with his body, and baits must be large. A
special feature of shark-fishing is the use of ground bait. This
is generally known as rubby-dubby, and consists of fish offals
and pieces of fish in a sack which is placed in the water to
attract the fish on to the feed. The scent from the bag spreads
out, funnelwise, and the roving, ever-hungry sharks gradually
swim in down this scented tunnel until they reach the baits –
and then – wham!
The *Blue Shark,* has a long pointed snout; it may run from
only a few pounds in weight (not much more than 20 perhaps) and is bluish in colour. Nonetheless, small though it
may be, it puts up a good scrap and is dangerous when being
landed and immediately after.
The *Porbeagle* is a faster fish than the blue shark and is much
larger. It is to be found chiefly in our western waters. Its chief

feature is the very disagreeable odour it gives off, so much so that it is the invariable practice to tow a captured porbeagle behind a boat and not bring it aboard!

The *Thresher* is also known as the Sea Fox. This is a very agile fish with an enormous tail fin, equal to its body in length. This shark leaves the water in spectacular and dangerous leaps and the thought of a large thresher crashing on to a small craft has before today caused the timid angler to cut the line and let the fish escape. An angling friend of mine, a professional photographer on a national daily newspaper, used to recall how he went to take photographs during a foray after sharks. He took a picture of an angler playing a thresher ten feet in the air!

The *Mako* – this is a ferocious fish from tropical waters which is a visitor to our shores. It may be that the coldness of our seas has kept it off man-eating – let's hope that it stays that way.

Dogfishes are not often sought after as a primary catch. They are not very sporting because they are voracious and easily taken, but when dogfishes are allowed in competition fishing, they are welcome because they often mean a win for an angler who would otherwise have been fishless.

From a commercial standpoint the dogfish is fairly valuable. His rough skin is used as the striker on boxes of matches and also as a 'sand' paper for wooden furniture manufacture. Its flesh is rather coarse, but it readily finds its way to fish and chip shops where, along with pollack and other fishes, it is sold under the names of 'flake' and 'rock salmon' – so now you know. Fertiliser manufacturers also use dogfishes in the making of manures. Though the larger sharks may be eaten, in fact shark steak is a good dish, the tope is comparatively useless but lobster fishermen gladly use its flesh as a bait for their lobster pots.

Shark's liver is rich in vitamins whilst the backbone of both tope and shark, which is not bone really but a form of cartilage, is often made into a walking stick as a worthy memento of a tough fight between angler and fish.

Tope fishing – this is a specialist pursuit indulged in by some sea anglers who very rarely go in for any other form of fishing.

Plate 5 (*opposite*) This ferocious shark was subdued by the girl angler.

Tope, too, often form the subject of special prizes during competitions and angling festivals both from shore and boats. But though tope fishing is a very specialised affair, it does not need the expensive or specialised equipment of the shark fisher.

A stout glass fibre 7-foot rod is ideal. The reel should be capable of taking at least 200 yards of 20 pounds breaking strain line, and the traces, which must be of wire, at least 6 to 7 feet in length. Hooks, at least 1 inch across the gape, complete the tackle.

The wire trace must be easily detachable by means of link attachments to both hook and line as it is impossible to remove the hook from a live tope without the risk of very serious injury from its dangerous teeth. The average tope is about 5 feet long and unless the trace is longer than the fish, when it is going straight away from the angler, one blow from its tail would sever the line as if it were knitting wool. The wire trace will also withstand the attacks from the tope's teeth.

A whole fresh fish, preferably a mackerel or herring, is used and the baited hook is allowed to drop to the sea bottom where it is allowed to remain stationary. Sometimes tope take if the bait is lifted slightly off the bottom by two or three turns of the reel handle.

A very surprising thing is the gentle way in which a tope approaches the bait: sometimes only the very faintest of tremors will indicate that a tope is interested, at other times the only signal is a plucking motion on the line. The time to strike is when the tope starts to make off after taking the bait: the fish will begin to strip line from the reel and then is the moment to strike. And strike hard.

Unlike some fish, the tope does not indulge in sudden swerves and dives and leaps, but makes strong, sustained rushes, and will often fight it out on the surface. The female tope is a bigger fish than the male, and of course puts up a much better fight. The tope is a gallant fighter and it is a great pity that so many are killed after capture: a modern school of thought, which is increasing, is that the tope should be returned to the sea unharmed after he has lost the battle.

The Skate

This is a large fish and though small fishes of about 20 pounds are taken by shore anglers, specimens of over 60 to 80 pounds are not uncommonly taken by boatmen. When hooked this fish uses its wide flat wings to keep itself free and it is difficult to move: this is where the pumping action described earlier comes in, and it becomes a trial of strength between angler and fish rather than exciting angling tactics.

The Ray

There are several of these in British waters. The chief and most important members are the Thornback and Sting Rays. The Sting Ray has a poisonous spine on its tail and this means extra care when handling it. Rays will take most baits, but fish baits must be fresh. At least 30 pounds breaking strain line is necessary and the rod and reel should be stout. As with the skates once the fish has been lifted it has to be pumped to the surface.

The Conger Eel

I think this is a grand fish. Specimens over 100 pounds in weight have been landed by professional boatmen and the average size of most conger taken is in the region of over 30 pounds. They may be caught from jetties, piers, rocks, and boats. But conger fishing from slippery rocks, especially in the night-time, can well be classed as a risky sport, for even a comparatively small conger can put up a powerful and determined fight, and in the excitement of the struggle, in the dark, on weed-slimed rocks, the conger can well get the angler off balance and throw him into the sea.

The best conger fishing is done from boats, and the best conger lairs are deep holes and old wrecks.

Conger eels prey on other bottom fish and are usually fished for on strong running leger tackle baited with fresh squid or cuttle. Mackerel, pilchard or herring can also be used. But in all cases the bait must be absolutely fresh because conger will not look at anything which is even slightly 'off'.

The hook must be attached to a wire link because the sharp teeth and strong jaws of the conger will prove too much for nylon. Sometimes cord is used for the trace as the softer material is not likely to cause a conger to reject the bait by finding a hard substance in his mouth. A cord, too, is easier to cut through when removing the hook from a *dead* conger: it is not recommended to attempt to remove a hook from a live one unless one wishes to lose a finger or even a hand: and there are thumbless and fingerless anglers to prove this point.

In addition to a wire or cord trace there should be 2 or even 3 swivels, as when a conger is hooked and being played he twists and spins deliberately.

It goes without saying that the whole tackle must be strong, and the hooks especially so. I have seen many a hook completely straightened out by a conger.

Leads can prove an expensive item from constant loss, and a piece of scrap iron or old nut and bolt attached to the tackle by a piece of cord is an excellent sinker. The cord should only have a few pounds breaking strain so that if it gets caught up in rocks or wreckage it is torn away without loss of line or hook.

If you are timid by nature don't go conger fishing! Especially at night. A conger, even a dead one, can inflict a nasty wound with its powerful jaws and it can tear the sole off an ordinary boot. The best way to secure a conger is to handline him ashore or into the boat and drop him into a sack tail first. A blow from a powerful conger could knock a man overboard, so watch his tail. It is advisable to try to stun the brute by bashing it hard with a cudgel over the vent and then cutting the spinal cord with a sharp knife or hatchet.

Congers are fairly good eating – and fried conger steak is next to halibut in my opinion. Conger also makes a good fish soup.

16　Fly Fishing

From the big game fish and their trials of strength and nerve, let us now turn to a delicate and artistic form of angling. This is fly fishing and may be practised not only against game fish, trout, salmon and sea trout, but amongst coarse fishes such as the chub, the rudd, the dace, and amongst sea fishes such as bass, mackerel, pollack, and coalfish. So fly fishing covers quite a wide area.

In freshwater fishing there are two methods of using the fly which is dressed, as it is termed, to represent a natural insect, or a stage in the life of a natural insect. In wet fly fishing the lure is submerged below the water surface and is generally used to explore the waters rather than to cast to a special fish. Dry fly fishing means that the fly floats on the water surface and this is cast to a particular fish which the angler has observed feeding. In dry fly fishing the artificial lure is dressed to as close an imitation as possible of the real thing on which the fish is actually feeding.

Flies are artificial lures. They consist of a hook dressed with materials such as silk, fur, feathers, to represent one of three stages in the life of an insect. There is not space in this book to describe fully these stages but briefly they are:

1. The larva stage, or as it may be called, the nymph stage
2. The sub-imago or intermediate stage when the flies have hatched out and known to the angler as 'Duns', and
3. The mature insect stage, or imago stage. In this condition they are termed 'Spinners'.

In the North of England they also call the 'Dun' stage 'Bloas'.

Fly fishing demands a special outfit. For the dry fly man it must be rather stiff: for the wet fly fisherman it may be fairly whippy. A special fly reel, on the centre-pin principle, is also used, and this is fastened to the butt of the rod at the base,

below the casting hand. A special line must also be used to match correctly the action and strength of the rod. The line should be tapered. The best fly lines, which can cost up to £5 and more will have a double taper: that is they have a heavy centre-section in their length which tapers to short lengths of smaller diameter at each end. This is to enable the fly angler to cast the correct distance with only a light fly on the line. There are usually two types of line on the market: one is solid dressed and the other has a hollow in it to help it float. The fly line is only about 30 yards long – this may surprise the average angler who is used to having two or three hundred yards of line on his spool, but the average fly fisher only casts from 15 to 20 yards. A good fly rod should be about 8 to 9 feet in length and the drum of the reel must be fairly large to allow for quick recovery of the line.

Of coarse fishes the dace rises freely to the fly, and the chub, often a good taker, nearly always chooses the most difficult spots in which to lie, generally beneath overhanging bushes. The rudd will take a fly, and also take bread paste on a hook fished in wet fly manner.

The trout is, of course, the most likely game fish with which a young angler is going to tangle. In some areas he may well begin fishing for trout, especially in the North of England and Scotland, long before coarse fish come his way.

The trout is to be found in lakes, reservoirs, large lochs, and rivers and streams. They are widely distributed and there are many ways of fishing for them, ranging from upstream worming to fly fishing. But fly fishing is, of course, the most socially recognised form.

There is no room in this book to describe the mechanics of fly fishing in detail but I think that the following notes on casting might be helpful. First of all one should practise 'dry', that is, in a field or parking lot where there is plenty of room. Assemble the rod and reel and line, but dispense with the cast and fly. Now remember the first rule which is: the rod must do all the work. Use only the wrist and forearm, not the shoulder.

Take up your position by standing easily, facing the direction you wish to cast. Relax. Hold the rod in front of yourself

Plate 6 (*opposite*) Fly fishing in fast water.

101

at an angle of about 45° with its own length of line hanging down from the top ring. Now pull off some line with the left hand until you have taken off about 8 feet, but hold this taut and yet ready to release it. Gently raise and lower the rod tip allowing the free line to work out so that finally it lies on the ground in front of you.

Now grip the rod with the thumb on top and pointing along the rod with the first finger below. Pull another yard of line off the reel and again hold it taut but ready for instant release. Waggle the rod to and fro until you can feel the line you are holding in the left hand trying to pull from your hold. When you can feel this pulling let it go and you will discover that the line will actually 'shoot' off. Keep on repeating this until you have about 7 or 8 yards of line out.

Keep practising this, bringing the line forward and backward until you can do it automatically. Now a new factor enters the scene – accuracy.

Place some object such as a plastic ring or plate on the ground and try to drop your fly on to it. When you can do this from 8 yards you can gradually increase the distance. You must not only practise in one direction but against the wind (and this will really give you a shock the first time you try it), across the wind, and with it. It is also a good idea to practise casting beneath obstacles such as bushes.

False casting, as this is termed, is also necessary not only to get line out but to dry a fly after it has been on the water. The main thing is to be smooth in all the actions and do not imitate the ringmaster at a circus, cracking his whip, otherwise you will crack the trace, cast and fly off your line.

The first attempts at casting flies to fish may well end in failure. The flow of the current must be studied and in a fast stream it is best, when casting across it, to cast too far and then check the line just before the fly drops. This overcomes the problem known as drag, which gives an unnatural motion to the lure.

When sea fishing with the fly, a pattern known as the Cuddy is often used. This is a large hook with a soft wool body on to which a pair of white hen feathers are wound. No special fly fishing rod is required for sea angling as fly fishing in the sea is more approximate to spinning. However, a light fly rod gives good sport with mackerel, but great care must be taken if using one to clean it extra carefully to get rid of the corrosive effects of the salt water.

17   Is Angling Cruel?

Somewhere, sometime, someone is going to tell you that fishing is cruel, and that it should be stopped. Today there is a great campaign going on against all forms of what are termed 'field sports' – that is, hunting and shooting, but angling also is included in the list of those pastimes which certain societies would like to see abolished.

Bigots on both sides, those against angling will say it is a cruel sport; the unthinking angler will promptly retort that it is not. Who is right and how does one judge cruelty?

First of all fishes are low in the order of living things so they do not feel fear and pain as higher creatures do: if a fish is properly hooked his only reaction is to try to get free, and if he does get free he will often come back to the bait and try to take it again.

But there are other things to consider. Suppose, and suppose only, that fishes do not undergo the feelings of fear and pain which human beings experience. None the less one must remember that fishes are living creatures and it is everyone's responsibility to see that unnecessary pain or suffering is not inflicted on them, nor is their resistance to disease decreased.

First of all, hooks. Now the hook is almost as old as man himself. Primitive hooks have always been equipped with barbs. But *today the barbed hook is completely out of date*. More anglers than ever are fishing: fishing waters are scarce: equipment has made angling simpler: and yet we stick to the primitive, prehistoric barbed hook. The barbed hook should not be included any longer in the list of angling equipment because if the angler is skilled enough he can catch, hold, and land his fish on barbless hooks.

Too often the barbed hook, if the strike is late, gets down

into the throat or even the stomach of a fish. This inevitably causes it some suffering, and usually results in death. If an angler is proud of his skill, and especially if he is a match fisherman, he should show that skill by using barbless hooks.

The treble and double hook, so often found on many artificial lures is a murderous item, and it is only old-fashioned conservatism which causes the manufacturer to go on churning out artificial lures with trebles and doubles on them. There is no place in modern angling for these relics of a barbarous past and they should be banned, if not by law, then by river and water authorities when issuing permits, or by clubs themselves writing such a ban into their own rules.

If enough anglers refuse to carry on these old-fashioned means of fishing, we should soon get good quality barbless hooks – I started campaigning in this field 2 years ago and so far have had quite a lot of support from angling sportsmen.

Not all anglers are skilled, by any means. Though one can write about, or teach, how to hook a fish correctly, and, even more important, how to unhook it and return it to the water, far too many anglers do this roughly. When a load of fresh fish was delivered to an English water an angling paper reported how nice it was to see them without the torn mouths and fins of their English counterparts, which had received such maulings from pleasure and competition fishermen.

No, angling is not cruel, as a sport. But there are thoughtless people who bring an element of cruelty into it. If fish are going to be retained for food, or as dead bait, then they should be killed immediately, either by breaking their necks (simply done in small fish by putting a finger into the mouth and with the thumb on the spine bending it back quickly) or by hitting it over the nose or head with a blunt instrument, or severing the spinal cord with a sharp knife. They should not be allowed to flop and flip about and die of suffocation out of water, either on the ground or stuffed alive into some bag or creel.

Keep-nets are completely unnecessary except for the actual competition which is being fished. The return of fish to the water does not disturb the fishing and the keep-net merely appeals to the gloating instinct of the captor. All too often fish get damaged by being crowded into keep-nets which are not sufficiently large, they lose scales and their protective slime coating. When they are returned to their natural element they should be released gently and not just tipped out or thrown back.

No wonder we are having outbreaks of fish disease – the poor fishes are all too often being captured several times during their lives (which shows that angling itself is not cruel) and each time they get such a handling that they become susceptible to parasites and diseases. Small fish which are to be returned to the water on capture should be released under the water surface, and not taken from that element. If a fish has to be handled to have the hook removed, then wet hands or a wet cloth should be used to hold it.

The stamping to death of small crabs by sea anglers on piers and promenades is unnecessary and though death is instantaneous and it cannot be classified as 'cruelty' none the less it does arouse hostile feelings in the hearts of spectators, as well as being anti-social and messy.

The large numbers of photographs taken of fish captured during a day's outing, though to be returned to the water without injury, does not do the fish any harm, provided the angler and photographer know their job. But, let's be perfectly honest, such pictures are sickening, and belong to a bygone era, when the wealthy sportsman posed with his foot on the head of some hapless beast he had shot.

The leaving of lengths of nylon on river banks and the shore is in itself a cruel practice, because this substance gets around the legs or wings of birds and other creatures and brings to them permanent injury, unnecessary suffering and hardship, and perhaps death.

Angling isn't cruel – but anglers can be. And it is not really so much deliberate cruelty as thoughtlessness which is responsible for some of the things I have described. I believe that the RSPCA have a good case against cruelty in many respects. Consider one rule which appears in many permits and the rules of water authorities and which reads something like this:

No person shall use any device or tackle that does not allow of the fish being taken therewith being returned to the water without serious injury.

106

Now that rule, of course, refers directly to spears and tridents, but equally well this could apply to the barbed hook, and I think a successful prosecution could be brought under this sort of rule where trebles are concerned.

There are also other considerations about angling besides cruelty. These are questions of behaviour at the waterside. Unfortunately, the hooliganish behaviour of some anglers has meant that waters have been closed to all anglers, good and bad alike. The breaking down of fences, leaving of litter and debris, lighting of fires, playing of loud radios and musical instruments, noisy behaviour, and insanitary practices are all too prevalent today. It is up to all anglers to set an example. To behave decently and responsibly and sportingly. It is on *everyone's* conduct that the future of angling depends.

Appendix

Fishing in fresh water is subject to licences and rules and conditions as to fish sizes, types of baits allowed and so on by River Authorities set up by Act of Parliament. I list below the addresses of the various River Authorities in England and Wales.

Avon & Dorset: Rostherene, 3 St Stephen's Road, Bournemouth, Hants.
Bristol Avon: Green Park Road, Bath, Somerset.
Cornwall: St Johns, Western Road, Launceston, Cornwall.
Cumberland: 256 London Road, Carlisle, Cumberland.
Dee and Clwyd: 2 Vicar's Lane, Chester.
Devon: County Hall, Exeter.
East Suffolk and Norfolk: The Cedars, Albemarle Road, Norwich.
Essex: Rivers House, 129 Springfield Road, Chelmsford, Essex.
Glamorgan: Tremaine House, Coychurch Road, Bridgend, Glamorgan.
Great Ouse: Elmhurst, Brooklands Avenue, Cambridge.
Gwynedd: Highfield, Caernarvon.
Hampshire: The Castle, Winchester, Hants.
Isle of Wight: County Hall, Newport, Isle of Wight.
Kent: Rivers House, London Road, Maidstone, Kent.
Lancashire: 48 West Cliff, Preston, Lancashire.
Lincolnshire: 50 Wide Bargate, Boston, Lincs.
Mersey and Weaver: Liverpool Road, Great Sankey, Warrington, Lancs.
Northumbrian: Dunira, 110 Osborne Road, Newcastle-upon-Tyne.
Severn: Portland House, Church Street, Great Malvern, Worcs.

Somerset: 12 King Square, Bridgwater, Somerset.
South-west Wales: Penyfai House, Penyfai Lane, Llanelly.
Sussex: 51 Church Road, Burgess Hill, Sussex.
Trent: 206 Derby Road, Nottingham.
Usk: The Croft, Goldcroft Common, Caerleon, Newport, Monmouthshire.
Welland and Nene: North Street, Oundle, Nr. Peterborough.
Wye: 4 St John Street, Hereford.
Yorkshire Ouse and Hull: 21 Park Square South, Leeds, 1.

Catchment Boards

Lee Conservancy: Brettenham House, Lancaster Place, Strand, London, W.C.2.
River Thames above Teddington Lock: Thames Conservancy, Burdett House, 15 Buckingham Street, London, W.C.2.

Index